20s/30s Ministry:
A Guide for Parishes

Nicholas E. Lombardo, O.P.

ISBN # 978-0-8091-5326-8

Paulist Evangelization Ministries
PO Box 29121
Washington, DC 20017

www.pemdc.org

©Paulist Evangelization Ministries, 2016   7650

Table of Contents

Important Information

Establishing a parish-based 20s/30s ministry can involve many issues of legal liability. Therefore, it is imperative that organizers respect civil laws and the guidelines of their parish and diocese, especially for activities that occur on parish grounds, or that involve the consumption of alcohol. Activities that involve the risk of physical harm, however minimal, should be organized with prudence. Furthermore, this guide is offered "as is", and no legal liability is accepted for problems that may occur in the course of implementing its suggestions.

Foreword

Now more than ever, the Church needs the presence and leadership of young adults.

Pope Francis, in his closing homily to the 3.7 million young adults gathered with him on Copacabana Beach in Rio de Janeiro for World Youth Day 2013, told them: "The Church needs you, your enthusiasm, your creativity and the joy that is so characteristic of you."

Through the ages, young adults have been so instrumental to the growth of Catholic faith and its impact on the world – from the young disciples of the Early Church to holy men and women of faith like Elizabeth of Hungary, Casimir Jagiellon, Aloysius Gonzaga, Kateri Tekakwitha, Charles Lwanga, Thérèse of Lisieux, Fr. Michael McGivney, and Pier Giorgio Frassati, among others.

Yet today, more and more young adults in their 20s and 30s are detaching from the practice of the faith and the community of the Church. A growing trend among the younger generations is the rise of the "nones," that is those who have no religious affiliation whatsoever. Studies show that over one-third of young adults in the United States are disconnected from any faith tradition, and even among self-identified Catholics, less than 17% of those in their 20s and 30s attend church on a weekly basis.

Faced with this daunting reality, how are we responding?

The bishops of the United States, in their pastoral plan for ministry with young adults, *Sons and Daughters of the Light* (USCCB, 1996), challenged church leaders in this regard, saying:

> **Our ministry with young adults...must be intensified.** We need to be a Church that is interested in the lives of these men and women and is willing to invite them into our community.

> We need to be a Church imbued with a missionary zeal for the Gospel. When young adults accept our invitation, we must welcome them, acknowledge their participation, and make room for them in all aspects of church life.

Since the late twentieth century, a variety of efforts have been made to engage and connect with men and women in their 20s and 30s – some have great success; but too often, most experience great struggle and declining numbers of young adults. Yet one of the key reasons why certain measures succeed is because the communities that support those efforts, and their leaders, invest time and resources into young adult outreach and ministry – and proactively and intentionally make a concerted effort to connect with those in their 20s and 30s within their community and beyond.

To respond to this reality, local communities cannot expect much change if their efforts or investment are minimal at best. This ministry cannot simply be handed off to well-intentioned people or the excitement of a few active young adults.

Pope Francis calls on the Church to form "missionary disciples," especially among Catholic young adults – so that they can go forth to the margins and the peripheries where their brothers and sisters are, compassionately and mercifully inviting their peers to journey with them to Christ and the Gospel.

Having an intentional 20s and 30s ministry – that both engages young adults as disciples and sends them forth into their world – is one way to respond to the call of the Holy Father and the bishops, and to the disconnection of so many people from active participation in the life of the Church. It is not the only way, but it is an effective step which communities can take to grow their engagement with young adults.

In the 1990s, the bishops of the United States said that "our ministry with young adults...must be intensified." In the twenty-first century, that urgency is even more apparent and necessary.

Young adults are truly a gift to the Church (as reinforced by St. John Paul II, who established World Youth Days as a way to illuminate their presence in the Universal Church). However, without these young men and women – and without a good and intentional ministry to connect with them and engage them in the practice of the faith – that gift may be lost.

The urgency of the present moment drives us to move forward in new and innovative ways, to "put out into the deep" and lower our nets for a catch. Yet the timeless invitation of Christ to all generations compels us to do this well and with a steady eye fixed on the Gospel and the Kingdom of God.

Father Nicholas Lombardo, O.P., has both thought about and worked with young adults across the United States. The fruit of his experience, gathered in this book, can provide an important structure for serving Catholics and others in their 20s and 30s as they explore their identity in faith and their vocation in the world. This book not only suggests a framework, but it also offers an adaptable and flexible model able to suit the specific needs of local communities.

Put out into the deep. Try something new. Give young adults an encounter with Christ that will transform them and, subsequently, transform the world.

Paul E. Jarzembowski
Assistant Director for Youth and
Young Adult Ministries
United States Conference of Catholic Bishops
Washington, D.C.
April 2016

Preface

This guide offers an adaptable, open-ended model for parish-based young adult ministry. It was written in wide consultation with young adults and young adult ministers from across the United States. It puts down in writing some of the best insights and practical suggestions that have emerged from the lived experience and trial and error of numerous young adults and young adult ministries.

This guide has come to be written through the contributions and suggestions of many different people, but most especially the young adults and staff of St. Gertrude's Parish in Cincinnati, Ohio, where I served as chaplain of its 20s ministry from 2005–07; various members of the Spirit and Truth organization, especially Lisa Fiamingo; some staff from the Archdiocese of Chicago, especially Dr. Timone Davis and Fr. Jordan Kelly, O.P.; Paul Jarzembowski, Assistant Director for Youth and Young Adult Ministries, USCCB Secretariat of Laity, Marriage, Family Life and Youth; and Fr. Frank DeSiano, C.S.P. Their contributions have been invaluable: their experience, their ideas, their materials and resources (especially the Spirit & Truth guide), and their generosity with their insight and feedback have been exceptionally helpful. To them, and to everyone who offered comments or suggestions on some draft of this guide, I would like to express my deep gratitude and appreciation.

Nicholas E. Lombardo, O.P.
Associate Professor
School of Theology and Religious Studies
The Catholic University of America
Washington, D.C.
April 2016

Introduction

Among Catholic young adults in the United States, there is widespread desire for authenticity in personal relationships, especially in one's relationship with God; interest in building strong communities; restless dissatisfaction with materialistic lifestyles; compassionate concern for the poor and afflicted; and resolute determination to grow in the knowledge and imitation of Christ. Having grown up well after the Second Vatican Council, Catholic young adults are less likely to view ecclesial controversies through an ideological lens. They tend to approach matters of faith with a spirit of freedom and creativity. For these reasons, this present moment is clearly a moment of special grace and opportunity for the Church and for young adults, with many signs of hope for the future.

As yet, however, the Church and its ministers, and Catholic young adults themselves, are only beginning to discover ways to harness these very positive indicators. Parish-based young adult ministry efforts provide one of the best ways forward. They unite Catholic young adults in Christ-centered communities. They also deepen young adults' connections to their parishes. By doing so, these ministries amplify the distinctive voice of Catholic young adults within the Catholic community, for the mutual benefit of everyone.

The need for parish-based young adult outreach is evident. Again and again, young adults say that they desire richer experiences of Christian community. Likewise, among Church leaders, there is widespread desire to welcome young adults more deeply into the life of their local parish communities. Parish-based young adult ministries respond directly to the felt needs of young adults as well as the Church's desire to incorporate young adults better into parish life. These communities are only one piece of the Church's ministry to young adults, but based on the experience of many young adult ministers, they are one of the most effective ways to draw young adults more fully into parish life. They are also one of the most effective ways to evangelize young adults on the margins, because they provide them an ongoing experience of Christian community with their peers, and not just one-time events or lectures.

This guide aims to give those interested in parish-based young adult ministry some ideas of where to begin drawn from the practical experience of many young adults and young adult ministers—and in so doing to facilitate the work of the Spirit in drawing together today's Catholic young adults more deeply into the Church's communion and the Church's service to the world.

The vision of this model of young adult ministry

The principal objective of this model of young adult ministry is to create a community of young adults that is closely attached to a parish, especially the parish's celebration of the Eucharist. This community is centered on a weekly meeting that usually includes Eucharistic adoration with contemporary music (although other forms of reflective prayer might be suitable in some circumstances), followed by discussion or an occasional lecture, and then socializing at a local bar or restaurant. This weekly meeting then becomes the anchor for a variety of other activities: social events, service, social justice outreach, sports, retreats, outdoor events, and whatever else people think up. The theological and pastoral orientation is one rooted in the teachings of the faith in a non-ideological, easy going manner that neither compromises the truth, nor beats people over the head, so that young adults of all backgrounds immediately feel welcomed and accepted.

The leadership of the ministry is provided by a core team of young adults who are assisted by a priest, pastoral leader, or advisor from the parish (in particular the parish staff). It is a consensus-based model that divides the decision-making and workload among a variety of young adults. In this way, it avoids putting the weight of responsibility on one or two young adult leaders. It also establishes a collegial context in which to negotiate the inevitable conflicts that arise. The involvement of a parish minister ensures that the ministry has a close connection to the parish and the universal Church, while the emphasis on the core team safeguards the creativity and independence of the young adults who provide the ministry's leadership and direction.

Finally, it should be emphasized that collegiality and adaptability lie at the heart of the 20s/30s model. The 20s/30s model of young adult ministry the fruit of networking and collaboration among young adults and young adult ministers. This model would never have come about if different ministries and individuals had not sought each other out to meet, discuss, and learn from each other. It is also intrinsically oriented toward incorporating new ideas and suggestions. Consequently, those using this model are highly encouraged to experiment with new formats and new ideas, but always in the context of the core team's deliberation and ongoing evaluation.

A word about scope and terminology

This guide does not offer suggestions for everything necessary to the Church's ministry to young adults. For example, it does not offer suggestions for making a parish young adult friendly in its liturgies and activities. It focuses instead on one crucial aspect of the Church's ministry to young adults: the creation and sustenance of parish-based communities of young adults.

Given its focus, this guide inevitably runs into an unresolved issue in young adult ministry: what should parish-based communities of young adults be called? In practice, parish-based communities tend to be called "groups," "fellowships," societies," or even just "communities." Many ecclesial ministers, however, are wary of using such words insofar as they can suggest exclusivity and separation. They suggest instead using words like "ministry" or avoiding any collective noun, opting for names like "St. Joseph's Young Adults" or "St. Joseph's 20-Somethings." The concern is that words like "group" and "fellowship" can subtly encourage participants to think of themselves as separate from the ordinary life of the parish, discourage openness to newcomers and infrequent attendees, increase the risk of cliquishness, and generally hamper its evangelical outreach. There is also concern that these words discourage young adults who are not already active in the Church from participating. Within the field of youth ministry, for example, great numbers of parishes refer not to the parish "youth group," but the parish "youth ministry."

Other ecclesial ministers, however, while sharing the same general vision of young adult ministry and the same general objectives, do not share these terminological concerns. Especially given the felt need of young adults for a sense of belonging, they see advantages to using words like "group" and "member." They are also concerned that words like "ministry" can sound like jargon and confuse and alienate unchurched young adults. Also, such words have a clear, non-charged meaning in both secular and ecclesial contexts, and for better or worse, they are widely used in both Catholic and Protestant communities.

As it takes shape, each new young adult ministry should give careful consideration to questions of terminology and how it wants to refer to itself. There are pros and cons for each possible option. As a placeholder, this guide refers to 20s/30s ministries, but it does not mean to prejudge a question that is based decided in view of concrete local circumstances.

Chapter 1

Overview of the Catholic 20s/30s Ministry

Mission statement

Looking at a sample mission statement adapted from an actual 20s/30s ministry is a good way to get an overview of the 20s/30s model. So here goes:

> The [Parish Name] 20s/30s ministry is a parish-based community of young adults, who seek to draw closer to Christ and his Church through prayer, friendship, discussion, study, and service. In addition to weekly meetings, we come together for a wide range of events: social gatherings, liturgies, service opportunities, athletic events, outdoor trips, retreats, conferences, etc. New participants from the parish and beyond (ages 20-39, single and married, Catholic and non-Catholic) are always welcome to join us for any meeting or event.

> We hope that young Catholics and other Christians will feel welcome to come and get to know us, and see the benefits of meeting and socializing with other young adults who seek to live their faith in the 21st century!

This sample mission statement captures the key elements of the 20s/30s model.

"Parish-based but open to all"

The 20s/30s ministry needs the home base of a particular parish for support and connection. As with any parish-based outreach, the connection should not be one way. Just as the ministry draws on the resources of the parishes, it should also be oriented to participating in weekend liturgies, parish programs, parish-organized service opportunities, *etc.*

This connection is not simply a matter of ecclesial justice. A living connection to a particular parish provides an important safeguard against spiritual narcissism. It also makes it easier to maintain a positive relationship to the larger Catholic community.

At the same time, the 20s/30s ministry should be open to young adults who are not members of the parish (or even regular churchgoers). Young adult communities typically require a critical mass of participants to thrive. One parish usually cannot supply enough young adults. In any case, if something good is happening, word will spread quickly, and young adults will inevitably be drawn to the ministry, often from great distances. Experience shows that young adults from outside the parish still benefit from the ministry's orientation to a particular parish. Young adults are attracted to the stability and grounded nature of a parish community. Inevitably, young adults find their involvement in their own parishes strengthened by the fact that the 20s/30s ministry is connected to the rhythms of parish life. Eventually, if the 20s/30s ministry grows enough, members of other parishes should be encouraged to start these communities in their home parishes. So the ministry needs to maintain a balance. On the one hand, the ministry as a whole should orient itself to its home parish. On the other hand, no one should feel that they need to choose between their home parish and the 20s/30s ministry.

In some situations, it may be preferable to have a regional 20s/30s ministry sponsored by a cluster of parishes, a deanery, or even a diocese. Even so, stable connections to particular parishes are advisable. (For more about regional 20s/30s ministries, see Chapter 7.)

"Community of young adults"

The primary purpose of a Catholic 20s/30s ministry is not a single activity, whether to evangelize or to catechize or to serve the poor or to encourage participation in Sunday Mass. The primary purpose is to create a community of young adults united in faith. It is important, therefore, that the ministry maintain a balance in its activities, in order to appeal to a wide variety of personalities and faith backgrounds. Generally what will happen is that each individual will be interested in certain activities and not others. Then, as friendships form and relationships grow, people will give other things a try. In the process, they often find that they like them more than they expected.

Many young adults seek a place where they are accepted, welcomed, and supported. If the community established by the 20s/30s ministry is truly invitational, pastoral, and compassionate, more and more young adults will be attracted to it. If a particular ministry does not regularly attract newcomers and especially young adults who are not already active Catholics, it may be a warning sign that the community is not adequately welcoming and supportive.

"Communion with Christ and his Church"

Ecclesial ministries cannot compete with the secular world when it comes to social events, sports, and other such activities. The secular world offers such activities "professionally," and it does a good job. However, a Catholic 20s/30s ministry offers something that the secular world by definition cannot offer: communion with Christ and his Church. For this reason, the 20s/30s ministry should highlight its religious and spiritual elements confidently and unabashedly (which is not to say unnaturally or obnoxiously), because it is precisely these religious and spiritual elements that nobody else has, sociologically speaking. Moreover, we know by faith that, regardless of how people respond to them in a particular time and place, these religious and spiritual elements are intrinsically attractive, and indeed the greatest source of authentic joy and happiness. More and more young adults today, including those less active in the practice of their faith, desire deep experiences of transcendence, peace, holiness, global justice, and mystery. This reality should inspire a certain confidence that what the Catholic 20s/30s ministry has to offer is good in itself, and that its religious dimension does not need to be downplayed in order to attract young adults. In fact, experience shows that it is just the opposite: Catholic young adult communities that downplay their religious or spiritual focus rarely thrive, precisely because they do not have anything distinctive to offer.

"Prayer, friendship, discussion, study, and service"

These elements seem to be the main elements necessary for a 20s/30s ministry to thrive. The health of the ministry will be jeopardized if any element is missing or—and this is an important point—emphasized disproportionately.

"Regular weekly meetings"

The anchor of the community is the regular weekly meeting, held on a weekday night. Wednesday or Thursday nights are ideal because they do not compete with weekends. They also provide a welcome break in the middle of the workweek. Although the ministry needs multiple meetings to thrive, the regular weekly meeting is the main meeting. Generally, it will also be the best attended. During this weekly meeting, the ministry should give special care to welcoming new participants. Care should also be taken to ensure that the evening's activities do not demand too much of newcomers: for instance, by becoming too personal, or by presuming too much intellectual knowledge of the faith.

The main elements of this regular meeting are threefold (as will be discussed in more depth later):

- ▶ An hour of Eucharistic adoration and contemporary music, with a brief homily. This time of prayer should be geared toward young adults, but open to the entire parish. Depending on the needs of the community, this time slot can be substituted with other forms of prayer or dropped entirely.

- ▶ An hour for discussion or a speaker, preceded by introductions, usually in a location other than the church. From here on, the meeting is only for the young adults.

- ▶ Departure for a restaurant/bar/coffeehouse or some other kind of social gathering, perhaps in the parish center.

Everybody is welcome to come to any or all parts of the evening. The schedule may need to be modified according to particular circumstances.

For this model to succeed to its fullest potential, this regular meeting must be weekly. Bi-weekly or monthly meetings are not frequent enough. Weekly meetings allow people to miss meetings without jeopardizing their connection to the community. Ironically, it often seems to happen that by having more frequent meetings, people come more often, with more commitment and more enthusiasm. The attraction of being part of a thriving community is such that people often start to restructure their other commitments, in order to be able to come more often. Frequent meetings create space for deeper friendships to take shape among ministry participants. These deeper friendships lead to increased excitement and commitment. Then the energy of these more active participants draws in young adults on the margins in a positive, reinforcing cycle.

"A wide range of events"

Besides the weekly meetings, there are other events: one-time events or gatherings, and other kinds of regular meetings. The one-time events include parties; service projects; special liturgies; camping trips; outings; retreats; mission trips; pilgrimages; etc. The regular meetings include bible studies; regular service commitments; monthly Sunday dinners; women's groups; men's groups; weekly ultimate Frisbee games; etc. In order to foster creativity, it is important that participants feel encouraged to experiment with new ideas.

"New participants from the parish and beyond are always welcome to attend any meeting or event."

It is essential that new participants feel personally welcomed when they start to attend meetings. The main weekly meeting always include introductions and some sort of icebreaker question. In this way, whenever new people show up, they immediately feel on equal footing with everybody else. Once a ministry is established, it is also good for the core team to plan special events with the particular goal of welcoming participants who have only recently started attending ministry meetings.

Care should be taken, however, that this welcoming not be forced or artificial. While it is important to make sure newcomers feel welcome, it is also important to avoid any inauthenticity in relationships, or any cult-like feel to meetings. Simply put, the ministry needs to make sure that it is oriented, in a natural way, to welcoming newcomers and making sure everybody immediately feels at home and valued. This welcoming orientation is a crucial dimension of the Catholic 20s/30s ministry community. Besides helping attract new participants, which is obviously critical to the ministry's long term success, it also helps the ministry avoid inwardness and cliquishness.

"Ages ??–??"

The Catholic 20s/30s model is specifically geared toward young adults in their 20s and 30s. In its pastoral plan for ministry with young adults, *Sons and Daughters of the Light* (1996), the United States Conference of Catholic Bishops writes: "young adulthood refers to people in their late teens, twenties, and thirties; single, married, divorced, or widowed; and with or without children." The 20s/30s model respects that framework in its approach to young adult ministry.

Each community, however, may need to settle on a specific age range for the primary focus of their ministry: for instance, ages 20-29, ages 20-35, or ages 20-39 are the most common designations. The question of a ministry's age range is very important. When a ministry is forming, it should give this matter careful consideration. [Chapter 6 discusses this question in depth.]

The question of age range closely relates to the problem of "aging-out," which is widely regarded as one of the most difficult problems in young adult ministry: what to do when participants "age out" of their ministry's designated age range. In general, communities need to find a way to balance fidelity to their mission with sensitivity to individuals older than their age range. Ministries that do not tackle this problem head-on tend to drift older and older, deterring younger adults in their 20s from participating in any significant numbers. [Chapter 11 discusses the issue of "aging-out" in more detail.]

"Single and married"

The Catholic 20s/30s ministry should welcome all young adults, and particularly married couples, who may be less likely to attend. As *Sons and Daughters of the Light* emphasizes, young adult outreach should include ministry to both singles and married couples. To this end (and especially for young adult parents), it is very helpful if the ministry can provide childcare, in order to foster the participation of single parents and married couples with children. Having married couples involved is win-win for the ministry: young married couples are often looking for peer communities, and singles benefit from their presence. Married couples model married life to their peers. They also bring a certain measure of stability to the ministry, since their very presence indicates that the ministry is not simply a way to meet a potential spouse. Still, most participants will probably be unmarried. Married couples, especially those with children, generally tend not have as much time for such a ministry.

"Catholic and non-Catholic"

It is important that, without compromising its Catholic identity, the ministry be welcoming toward both Catholics and non-Catholics (as well as inactive Catholics and those with no religious affiliation), especially because non-Catholic participants are likely to attend on any given week. This can be done in a natural way by being especially attentive to framing faith discussions in ways that emphasize the positive. This allows for open discussion of even distinctively Catholic beliefs that would be controversial among other Christians (say, the nature of the Eucharist or the role of the Pope, *etc.*) without running the risk of seeming disrespectful to the beliefs of non-Catholics. The group may also want to discuss ecumenical or interreligious themes now and then. This ecumenical sensitivity will also make it easier for Catholics who have difficulty with particular Church teachings to feel welcome and included, and as a result perhaps even give those very teachings another look.

Website and social media description

Many young adults will likely hear about a Catholic 20s/30s ministry for the first time on the internet and through social media. It is important, therefore, that the home page and the social media page give a concise and welcoming description of the ministry.

Here is a sample online description adapted from an actual Catholic young adult ministry that incorporates the sample mission statement on their website:

Welcome!

The [Parish Name] *20s/30s ministry is a parish-based community of young adults who seek to draw closer to Christ and his Church through prayer, friendship, discussion, study, and service. In addition to weekly meetings, we come together for a wide range of events: social gatherings, liturgies, service opportunities, athletic events, outdoor trips, retreats, conferences, etc. New participants from the parish and beyond (ages 18–32, single and married, Catholic and non-Catholic) are always welcome to join us for any meeting or event.*

We hope that young Catholics and other Christians will feel welcome to come and get to know us and see the benefits of meeting and socializing with other young adults who seek to live their faith in the 21st century!

What we're about!

Our ministry originated from several young adults in the parish who were seeking fellowship and spiritual growth with other young Christians. The ministry was founded in [Month, Year] and has been growing and developing ever since.

Our main weekly meeting is on [Day of Weekly Meeting] *nights at* [Parish Name] *Church. From 7–8 pm, we gather in the church for Eucharistic adoration and contemporary music. From 8–9 pm we meet in the parish center for a discussion or speaker. Afterwards we head out to a bar/restaurant or have some kind of gathering at the parish center. Everybody is welcome to come to any or all parts of the evening. Other meetings and events are planned throughout the week.*

The focus of our ministry is twofold. On the one hand, we seek to foster a lighthearted spirit and an enjoyable and friendly atmosphere. On the other hand, we are serious about deepening our communion with Christ and his Church in a society that sometimes challenges our faith. Thus, we hope to combine fellowship with prayer and faith in order to promote an open, vibrant Christian culture, and the mutual encouragement of Christian life among participants of the ministry.

We strive to reach young adults in their twenties through prayer, study, service, fellowship, faith sharing and friendships. Each individual brings unique gifts and talents to the ministry. Our ministry continues to flourish because of the new addition of young adults with varying talents, personalities, backgrounds and experiences. It is always exciting to see so many new faces each week. We hope you feel welcome to join us!

The Core Team

Overview

The administration and governance of the Catholic 20s/30s ministry is provided by a core team of young adult volunteers. The core team is assisted by a chaplain and/or a lay advisor (who should be older than the age range of the ministry). Leadership responsibilities do not rest on any single individual. Some core team members have particular responsibilities. Others simply participate in core team meetings and volunteer to assist with occasional events. (See Appendix A for a complete listing of various functions of the core team and more detailed descriptions.)

The core team meets monthly. These monthly meetings are led by the secretary or ministry coordinator. Decisions are made by consensus through a process of conversation and discussion, and votes are taken only when necessary. If the ministry has a budget, the core team oversees the distribution of funds.

To minimize competition and encourage a cooperative spirit, elections are avoided whenever possible. No position other than ministry coordinator should be elected. In fact, it can be preferable to avoid electing the ministry coordinator: instead, the chaplain or older lay advisor can collect nominations from community, and afterwards appoint the ministry coordinator. In any case, however the ministry coordinator is selected, the remaining positions are not elected. They are filled at an annual meeting by consensus, in a way that will be explained below. Moreover, to foster transparency and common ownership, any young adult active in the ministry should be welcome to join the core team as a member-at-large, and to do so at any time.

The core team agrees upon some sort of written description of its internal governance. Then this written description is posted on the ministry's website for all to read.

Description of the core team
(should be posted on ministry website and social media)

The leadership of the 20s/30s ministry is provided by a core team of young adults and its chaplain and/or advisor. The core team organizes meetings and events and makes policy decisions. However, the core team welcomes feedback and suggestions from the entire 20s/30s ministry. It is a non-elected body, composed of those interested in giving their time to organization and leadership.

Conscious that "if the Lord does not build the house, in vain do its builders labor" (Ps 127:1), the core team's first priority is developing and maintaining authentic communion with Christ and each other. In this spirit, members seek to pray for each other and help carry each other's burdens—in all things, "striving to preserve the unity of the spirit through the bond of peace" (Eph 4:3). Core team members should resolve any disagreements promptly, according to the guidelines laid out by Christ in Matthew 18:15-20, so that these disagreements serve rather than harm the ministry's communion.

The core team meets regularly. Anybody interested can join at any time by contacting the core team ministry coordinator.

Organizational principles
(should be posted on ministry website and social media)

The following are the principles that should guide the core team:

> ▸ As the core team discusses various options, the goal is consensus rather than sheer majority rule. Therefore the discussions should be oriented toward proposals that recognize everybody's concerns, and solutions that are

both/and rather than *either/or*. Yet when important decisions must be made, and discussion is at an impasse, matters will need to be resolved by a vote. Even then, though, charity should guide the proceedings. This consensus-based model ensures that the core team moves ahead as a unit. It also inspires proposals that nobody would have thought of individually.

▸ All major decisions are the prerogative of the entire core team. Consequently, important proposals, ideas, and concerns should be raised with the entire core team. Minor matters can be handled by the appropriate individual or committee.

▸ In the core team's discussions, decisions, and event-planning, the chaplain or advisor may need to exercise some oversight, especially in the light of pastoral concerns or other activities going on in the parish.

▸ Every decision made at a core team meeting should have someone assigned to take charge of its implementation.

▸ To avoid burn-out, core team members should always feel free to step back either temporarily or indefinitely, whenever their responsibilities start to feel burdensome, or something comes up in their lives that demands their attention.

▸ The core team meets every month. When possible, an agenda should be distributed a few days beforehand, and minutes sent out within a week.

▸ Core team members serve for a period of one year.

▸ Every year the core team will undertake a process of reflection and evaluation to consider how the ministry is doing. The purpose of this self-evaluation is to take stock of what is going well, and also to see if there are any areas that need improvement, and if so, how to set about the necessary improvements.

How core team positions are assigned

All positions are voluntary. Once a year, the main weekly meeting is given over to a discussion of the core team by its current members. Everybody describes their position, and what they actually do on the core team. At this meeting, the 20s/30s core team members are asked to consider prayerfully taking a role on the core team.

Selecting the ministry coordinator

The 20s/30s ministry coordinator can be selected either by election or appointment. Either way, the process of selection begins by collecting nominations. Nominations are collected over a period of a couple weeks. Members are encouraged to nominate themselves. If the coordinator is selected by election, the core team secretary collects the nominations, asks each nominated person whether they would be willing to serve as ministry coordinator, and then conducts the election during one of the weekly meetings. If the coordinator is selected by appointment, nominations are sent to the chaplain or advisor. During this time, the chaplain or advisor prays for guidance from the Holy Spirit and considers the nominees. Then the chaplain or advisor asks somebody if he or she is willing to serve as coordinator for the coming year. If that person accepts, he or she is the new ministry coordinator.

Ministries may also want to develop a co-leader framework, where two young adults serve together and divvy up tasks between themselves. This approach also allows for more consensus-based decision making and avoiding the appearance of the ministry being one person's personal project. Another advantage is that, if new commitments arise for one of the coordinators, the other coordinator can easily step up. It might also be worthwhile to consider a staggered term between the two coordinators, to ensure continuity and institutional memory on the part of the ministry leadership.

All other positions

Shortly after the coordinator (and/or co-coordinator) is selected, a special meeting of the core team is held to fill all other positions. This special meeting is open to anybody who is interesting in being involved in the core team. Individuals volunteer by writing down on a sheet of paper those position(s) in which they would be willing to serve for the coming year. If individuals are interested in more than one position, they should volunteer for all of them. The papers are tallied simultaneously, and the results noted on newsprint or a marker board. (This process makes it easier for people to state their true preferences. Because the self-nomination is simultaneous and secret, people feel freer to state their honest preferences. Otherwise, people tend to be silent if someone else indicates interest in a particular position first.)

If there is more than one volunteer for a given position, either someone will need to withdraw his or her name, or else they can serve together. But if multiple persons decide to serve together, they should select one person to be the main contact for that role, with the rest serving as committee members. If no one volunteers for a given position, core team members present at the annual meeting are given an opportunity to step forward. In the absence of any such volunteer, the new ministry coordinator advertises the empty positions among the entire 20s/30s ministry until they are filled. Sometimes, however, the lack of interest in a certain position can indicate that the ministry no longer needs that position, and that it should be dropped.

Due to the risk of burn-out and overwork, one person should not take on multiple core team positions, except in cases of strict necessity.

Members-at-large

Members-at-large are members who participate in core team meetings without having any particular position or responsibilities. Anyone can become a member-at-large at any time simply by contacting the ministry coordinator and attending core team meetings.

Small group discussion leaders

Small group leaders are needed to lead discussions at the weekly meeting. They need not attend core team meetings if they do not wish to do so. The core team may want to arrange for small group leader training occasionally throughout the year. A member of the parish staff may be able to assist with this training.

Annual review

Every year, midway through its term of service, the core team may want to undertake a general review of how things are going. First surveys are distributed to the ministry with few general essay questions (see appendix for a sample survey), either by paper or by email. One of the core members collates the responses. Then core team members meet once or twice for the purpose of discussing the surveys. During these annual meetings, core team members offer their own thoughts on how things are going, and discuss how to go about addressing any concerns that have been raised.

Occasional planning retreats

The core team may also find it beneficial to arrange a day-long planning retreat from time to time to build community and clarify its objectives. Such planning retreats are especially helpful when a ministry is first starting up. Although such planning retreats can be held on parish grounds, it is often preferable to go somewhere different. The core team may want to contact local religious order communities to see if they may be able to host a day long gathering. The planning retreat should include time for prayer and reflection as well as discussion.

The Weekly Meeting

Overview

The main weekly meeting has three parts: (1) a period of prayer, typically (but not necessarily) Eucharistic adoration; (2) faith discussion or presentation; (3) social gathering, usually at a local restaurant/bar/coffeehouse. Ministries should feel great freedom to improvise based on particular circumstances. Since the weekly meeting is central to the life of the ministry, however, adjustments to its format should always be made with great care. They should also be made with a strong consensus among core team members.

> n.b. This chapter provides many suggestions that have proven effective in concrete experience. Particular ministries may or may not want to follow every suggestion.

Elements of a successful weekly meeting

Open-ended participation

All young adults should feel encouraged to come to any or all of the three-parts of the evening. There should be no sense that people are obliged to come for the entire evening.

Accessible and welcoming atmosphere

The weekly meeting serves as the spiritual and social anchor for an intentional community of Catholic young adults. It also the most natural point of entry for new participants. These two functions of the weekly meeting should always be kept in mind. Consequently, when planning the weekly meeting, core team members should ask themselves these sorts of questions: Would adopting a certain regular practice over-emphasize a particular spirituality and marginalize those who do not share it? Would newcomers find a particular evening's meeting welcoming? Might newcomers find some aspect uncomfortable?

Variety in faith discussion

Every weekly meeting involves some kind of faith discussion. Variety is important. Any single format, no matter how excellent, can become stale. For example, discussion based on the Gospel of the day can be very posi-tive. However, if the same thing happens week after week, it can become tedious and rote, especially for those who would be more interested in hearing a guest speaker from time to time, or in discussing theology. Variety makes the faith discussion portion of the meeting more interest-ing. It also serves the needs of different kinds of people, who each have different preferences. Variety should not become an end in itself, how-ever. Some stability is also important, so that people have some idea of what to expect.

Positive tone

The purpose of the faith discussion is to give participants an opportunity to reflect on their lives, grow in insight, and deepen their knowledge of the faith. It aims to create a setting in which they can mutually encourage each other in the faith and grow in their comfort in talking about their faith. It should be emphasized that the meeting is not about hashing out theological fights or proving people wrong. Coordinators need to set a tone of reflective searching for insight and wisdom.

Low maintenance format

The actual weekly meetings must be relatively low maintenance for the organizers. Otherwise, the workload will quickly lead to burn out. In any case, if the weekly meetings do require a great deal of planning, they are probably over-programmed: young adults generally prefer things that are more free-flowing.

Delegation of organization to multiple individuals

Ideally, each portion of the weekly meeting should be the responsibility of a different person. For instance, the music ministry, the adoration set-up, and each different faith discussion format should each have a different person in charge. This approach ensures that multiple people feel ownership of the weekly meetings, and it avoids overburdening any single individual. This division of labor may not be possible for ministries that are just starting out, but it is a good thing to strive toward.

Eucharistic adoration and prayer

Overview

Eucharistic adoration (or another form of prayer that fosters recollection and contemplation) is the first portion of the weekly evening. A period of relaxed, contemplative prayer allows people to unwind after a day of work and connect with God. Afterwards, people tend to be refreshed and cheerful, which in turn leads to more vital and interesting discussions. It also serves a very practical function: this period of prayer allows those who arrive late to drift in without embarrassment and without disruption. Experience suggests that adoration time lasting one hour works very well, but a full hour may not be possible or preferable in all settings. (Note: according to particular needs and circumstances, individual ministries may want to substitute or omit this period of prayer.)

Adoration and music

If Eucharistic adoration is chosen as the prayer form, a crucial element of this period of the gathering will be the use of contemporary music (and most typically, but not necessarily, praise and worship music). Some young adults may enjoy or even prefer silence, and others may prefer traditional hymns, the Liturgy of the Hours, or the rosary. Yet the use of contemporary music is essential for the adoration portion to have a broad appeal, especially among young adults who are on the margins of Church life. It also adds an element of energy to the prayer which has a positive impact on the subsequent discussion and social gathering. On occasion, it may be helpful or necessary to substitute something else in place of contemporary music, but these substitutions should be infrequent.

This does not mean that more traditional aspects of Eucharistic adoration should be excluded. In fact, it is beneficial if this period of adoration integrates some traditional hymns such as *Adoro Te Devote*, *O Salutaris*, or *Tantum Ergo*, in English or Latin. Including these elements acquaints young adults with some of the Church's traditions in a natural way. It also makes it easier for young adults to transition to more standard parish events down the road.

If another prayer form or devotion is used, the same principles on the integration of music apply. Music is a helpful way for young adults to enter into the contemplative experience of prayer.

Connection to larger parish community

Some parishes have extended periods of adoration during the week. It is ideal if the weekly meeting can be timed to overlap with the last hour of the day's adoration, in order to integrate the ministry more into the life of the parish. This provides a twofold benefit. First, it makes the ministry more conscious of its connection with the parish. Second, older parishioners feel more welcome to attend (many of whom also enjoy this style of adoration, and find praying with young adults encouraging and inspiring).

Suggested structure for adoration

A typical period of adoration lasts for one hour and might look something like this:

▸ Exposition (with G. M. Hopkins English translation of the *Adore Te*)

▸ Two or three contemporary songs, ideally accompanied by guitar and keyboard

▸ Brief period of silence

- ▶ The priest or deacon reads the Gospel of the day and gives a short reflection
- ▶ Period of silence
- ▶ Two or three contemporary songs
- ▶ Benediction, with *Tantum Ergo* in Latin
- ▶ Divine Praises, followed by *Salve Regina* in Latin
- ▶ Final contemporary song

Sometimes it may happen that no musician is available. On such occasions, the contemporary songs can be substituted with silence, the Liturgy of the Hours, or the rosary. If silence is chosen, sheets with intercessory prayer intentions may be distributed, so that people, if they so choose, can pray silently for those intentions. Lists of prayer intentions for other young people can be particularly helpful and meaningful. (See the appendices for sample lists of prayer intentions.)

Alternatives to Eucharistic adoration

During the weekly meeting, some ministries may wish to use a form of prayer besides Eucharistic adoration, either regularly or occasionally. In general, whatever form of prayer is chosen, it should be ordered to foster contemplation and recollection. Care should also be taken to make it accessible to everyone. Alternative possibilities include: *lectio divina*, Liturgy of the Hours (especially Vespers), Taize prayer, silent contemplative prayer, praise and worship music, recitation of the rosary, Stations of the Cross (especially in the season of Lent), the Divine Mercy chaplet, a litany, and the Ignatian Examen. It is best to work with the local parish (or regional or diocesan) leadership to see what options may be available. They may able be able to assist in developing an effective and prayerful experience for the young adults in attendance.

Another possibility is to connect with a religious community in the area with a particular charism (for example, Benedictines are known for their practice of *lectio divina*) who might be open to leading or coordinating the prayer on a regular basis.

The beginning of the faith discussion

Overview

The faith discussion is the second segment of the meeting. Typically, after adoration or prayer, young adults walk from the church to somewhere else on the parish grounds where a meeting can take place, with chairs set up in a circle (or, if there will be a talk, with chairs set up facing the speaker). This segment includes a welcome; introductions and an opening prayer; a talk or small group discussion; and then announcements and a closing prayer.

The welcome, introductions, and opening prayer

Every meeting, without exception, begins with introductions. The opening of the meeting runs like this:

> The 20s/30s ministry coordinator (or co-coordinator) starts the meeting and welcomes those present. If the coordinator (or the co-coordinator) cannot be present for this gathering, he or she delegates somebody else to lead the meeting.

> The ministry coordinator (or their designate) invites those gathered to introduce themselves, and then answer some random question, *e.g.*, what is your favorite picnic food, what was the last book you read, favorite childhood cartoon, *etc.* (see appendix for more suggestions). This sort of introduction opens the meeting in a light hearted way, without making those who are shy feel like they have to say anything particularly revealing. The importance of this opening introduction cannot be overemphasized. It gives participants and newcomers a chance to inject their personality into the meeting and to get to know each other. It makes newcomers feel immediately at home. It also sets the right tone for the spirituality of the ministry: fully human and fully alive. (Note: Although this model does not advocate using nametags, due to the more formal atmosphere they generate, many young adult ministries do find them helpful. Some

ministries, for example, exchange nametags at the end of the meeting and pray for that person during the coming week.)

> **n.b.** If there will be a long talk that evening, or if something special is planned that requires more time, the introductory question chosen should prompt simple, short answers. It is not omitted, however, except for the most exceptional reasons.

Afterwards the coordinator leads the meeting in a brief prayer and introduces the next part of the meeting.

If the numbers are large, and there is a small group discussion, people break up into smaller groups (ideally around 6-9 per group). Rather than asking people to form their own groups, the coordinator invites people to count off (1, 2, 3, 1, 2, 3, *etc.*) so that everybody ends up meeting new people.

The faith discussion's rotating format

The format changes every week on a monthly rotation:

Week One: Presentation

Week Two: Scripture Discussion

Week Three: Reflection and Discussion

Week Four: Theology Discussion

Week Five: Open Format

The rotation should not be seen as an iron-clad structure. It is a rough organizational guide that should be adapted according to preference and necessity. For example, a speaker may only be available for a presentation on the third week, and so the schedule that month will need to be adjusted. The key thing is to rotate the format from week to week.

> **n.b.** The Scripture Discussion is often the easiest meeting format to prepare, and so it is a good option when other things fail, as when it happens that a speaker cancels at the last minute, or there is difficulty coming up with a format for a 5th meeting.

Week One: Presentation

Overview

This week's format offers an extended presentation on a theological topic, possibly followed by a question and answer period. Speakers and topics are decided in advance by a committee and/or the individual delegated by the core team to be in charge. Topics can range over any topics, from anything from the Trinity, to Scripture, to moral theology, to social justice, to ecumenical or interreligious matters, to prayer and liturgy, to vocations and marriage, to young adult culture and ministry, to practical insights into living the faith every day, but topics should always be chosen with attention to the needs and concerns of young adults. The purpose of these presentations is to give an opening to the intellectual treasures of the Catholic tradition. They are not meant to provide a complete theological education. Rather, they are meant to give people a taste of new perspectives and new insights, and to inspire people to deepen their knowledge of the faith on their own.

Selection of speakers and topics

The presentation topics are chosen by a committee for a six-month period. The committee brainstorms for topics and speakers. Then, after coming to some determination about the ranking (with some alternates, in case certain lectures cannot be scheduled), it is left to the Presentation Coordinator to schedule the sessions. Speakers may be drawn from the parish or beyond. If the ministry has a budget and it is feasible, a modest stipend may be offered to speakers who come from outside the parish. The chaplain and/or advisor should be involved in the discussion about presentation topics and speakers, as they may have important pastoral insights. Even if they cannot be involved in the discussion, the chaplain and/or advisor should always be consulted before the ministry finalizes its slate of presentations.

The selection of speakers and topics is very important. There is great potential for good as well as bad. Any given speaker or topic may not greatly impact the ministry, but the *pattern* of speakers and topics plays an important role in shaping the ministry's identity. If the speakers are well-publicized (which may or may not be desirable), then the pattern of speakers and topics will also shape the ministry's *public identity*. For this reason great care should be taken in the scheduling of the presentations.

Theological orientation

To ensure that it reaches the greatest number of young adults, the 20s/30s ministry should seek to present the teachings of the Church and the Second Vatican Council without an agenda of any kind. Speakers should likewise be chosen who manifest a similar commitment to both fidelity and pastoral sensitivity. For those presentations addressing aspects of moral theology, it is strongly encouraged that they be **virtue-centered** rather than **obligation-centered**. Similarly, where appropriate, the call to holiness should be the central message, rather than the related but subsidiary call to avoid sin. In sum, the focus should be more on how the Christian life leads to human excellence and happiness, and less on commandments and laws, without of course neglecting their importance. Not only is this is good theology, it is particularly helpful and attractive to young adults. It is also an important element of the New Evangelization: often Christians know *what* the Church teaches about morality, but they do not understand *why*, and this approach helps Christians to see how the Church's teachings lead to happiness.

Week Two: Scripture Discussion

Overview

This week's format is a faith discussion based on a common scriptural text. Typically the Gospel of the day is discussed in small groups in response to some prepared questions.

Selection of Scripture texts

Many texts would be appropriate for the discussion, and ministries should feel great freedom in their selection of texts. Readings may be drawn from the liturgy. Alternatively, the ministry can gradually work through a particular book of the Bible.

There are advantages, however, to choosing a reading from the liturgy of the day, and especially the Gospel of the day. It connects the ministry with the liturgy of the universal Church. It also connects with the preceding adoration, since the priest or deacon typically reads and preaches about the Gospel of the day. Moreover, Gospel texts generally lead to discussion more easily, because they are always explicitly Christ-centered, and tend to be more concrete. Using the readings of the day rather than the coming Sunday grounds the ministry in the present moment. It also exposes participants to a wider range of texts then they might encounter just attending Sunday Mass. Having said that, some ministries may find it preferable to use the Sunday readings for the discussion. Even for ministries that normally use the readings of the day, for certain seasons like Advent and Lent, choice of the upcoming Sunday readings can be a good option because of the way they further the particular spiritual disposition which the season is encouraging. It allows participants to put their pre-Christmas busyness, for example, into a more spiritual context.

Preparing the discussion questions

Experience shows that prepared questions about the reading are very helpful for prompting discussion. It is helpful to have a combination of "general purpose" questions and then specific questions that have been prepared for that evening's reading. Each question should direct participants to discuss their faith and their experiences in the light of that day's particular Scripture passage. They should guide the conversation toward people's own understanding of the text, and its relevance to their lives. The discussion questions should not require any special knowledge of Scripture. That would shift the discussion toward "factual" questions, and away from people's lived experience of the faith. It would also make those less knowledgeable feel uncomfortable about contributing to the discussion. Few people are experts on Scripture or theology, but everybody is an expert on his or her own experiences and his or her own understanding of the faith. For example, "What do Christ's words in this passage mean for us today?" is a more helpful discussion question than, "What is the difference between a Pharisee and a Sadducee?" Depending on interests, people may end up talking about the difference between Pharisees and Sadducees, and that can be very good, but the questions should not set out to encourage this sort of discussion.

Small group leaders

The small group discussions are led by volunteers from the 20s/30s ministry. These volunteers put themselves "on-call" to lead discussions during weekly meetings. Then, at any given meeting, the ministry coordinator asks the small group discussion leaders present to raise their hands, and he or she picks some of them for that week's meeting. Then each small group discussion leader is given a sheet with the day's Gospel and the prepared discussion questions.

Personal introductions when there are small group discussions

Part of the purpose of faith discussion portion is to enable young adults to get to know each other better. Therefore, it is important that a second round of introductions always precede the small group discussion. It is helpful to ask people to say more than just their names. For instance, the small group discussion leader might invite people to mention a high and/or low of the past week.

Suggested guidelines for small group leaders

▶ Begin with introductions and "highs & lows" (that is, sharing a "high" and "low" of the past week).

▶ Have somebody read the Scripture passage.
 Ask people not to read along, but to listen to the reader.

▶ Allow for a brief period of silence.

▶ Go around the group and ask everybody to say what spoke to them and why. One is always free to "pass."

▶ Ask those prepared questions that seem right. Feel free to add your own.

▶ Do not be afraid to allow extra silence before moving on to the next question; sometimes people take their time before contributing to the discussion. The discussion should not feel "rushed" from question to question.

▶ As the time draws to a close, you may want to offer intercessions. There are many ways to do this. One way is to name a need and finish by saying, "We pray to the Lord" and the others will naturally respond "Lord, hear our prayer." People may also want to address God or the saints directly. People should feel free to pray as long as they want, and not just to raise petitions, but to offer prayers of praise and thanksgiving as well.

▶ Close with a standard prayer that everybody is likely to know, such as the *Our Father*, *Hail Mary*, or *Glory Be*. Alternatively, another prayer, especially psalms or traditional Catholic prayers, can be printed on sheets and prayed in common. You may want to introduce this common closing prayer with your own spontaneous prayer.

Week Three: Reflection and Discussion

Overview

In the reflection and discussion format, a young adult shares some personally experienced insight into the faith. Afterward there are small group discussions.

Content

This format gives a forum for personal reflection on a particular faith-related topic, in the light of personal experiences and the teachings of Christ and his Church. It is neither a lecture, nor an unfocused sharing of personal experiences. For example, a reflection might focus on prayer; a particular sacrament; God's providence; Christ's teaching on forgiveness; the struggles of remaining faithful in the light of pressures or temptations; serving Christ in the poor; finding God in the community of the Church; working for justice; the communion of saints; *etc.* From time to time, young adults may feel called to speak about the story of their conversion or how they came to a deeper faith. That is certainly appropriate and to be encouraged. However, such talks should be the exception, not the rule.

These reflections can and should be personal. At the same time, speakers should be wary of sharing too much personal information. When questions arise, speakers should consult with the reflection coordinator or other core team members to ask for feedback about what would be appropriate.

> **n.b.** Some may prefer to call these reflections something like "testimonies" or "witness talks." The key point is that these reflections should focus more on the living out of the Christian discipleship in ordinary life rather than a story of conversion and/or commitment to Christ. Many people, however, associate the idea of testimonies and witnessing with stories of personal conversion. For that reason, they are called here reflections.

Selection and preparation of speakers

The reflection coordinator is responsible for asking for volunteers. These volunteers may choose to speak on any theme. After a volunteer has come forward, the coordinator speaks with him or her about the content of the talk. At some point they should go over the talk together, in order to help the volunteer feel more encouraged and confident, and also to address any obvious problems.

It is important that volunteers talk to somebody before presenting their reflections. This will prevent any glaring problems. It will also protect the volunteer from revealing too much, insofar as those who have not spoken about their faith in public before may reveal more about themselves than is appropriate. If the coordinator has reservations about whether a particular volunteer should address the community, the ministry coordinator, chaplain, and/or advisor should be consulted. Sometimes it may be necessary to ask for the volunteer to choose a different topic, or to wait a while before speaking, but this should always be done with great sensitivity and gratitude for their offer.

Structure

The following is the basic structure of the reflection and discussion format:

- ▶ Brief introduction of the talk's topic
- ▶ Reading of some relevant passage from Scripture
- ▶ Discussion of the talk's topic via reflections on one's personal experiences and insights, with some attention to how they relate to the teachings of Scripture and/or the Church.

After the talk, people break up into small groups and discuss.

Scripture passage

The talk should begin with a reading of a brief Scripture passage chosen by the speaker. The passage is important for two reasons. First, it encourages the speaker to connect his or her talk with Scripture. Second, it provides a concrete point of reference for discussion afterwards, making it is easier to discuss the topic without feeling obligated to comment on the speaker.

Suggested length

Talk should aim to be 10–15 minutes long in order to leave sufficient time for discussion. The upper limit for a talk is 20 minutes. If a speaker antici-pates going this long, he or she should talk this over with the reflection coordinator beforehand.

The discussion afterwards

After the reflection, the young adults break for small group discussion on some prepared questions. The discussion questions should be focused on the topic and the Scripture passage, but not the speaker's talk. This avoids putting people on the spot and asking them to agree or disagree with what the speaker said. People should be free to comment on the speaker's presentation, but they should not feel forced to do so either.

The reflection coordinator is responsible for developing the discussion questions and distributing a handout to small group discussion leaders. The speaker is welcome and encouraged to prepare discussion questions for the reflection coordinator, but the speaker may or may not want to do so, and it is ultimately the reflection coordinator's responsibility.

Week Four: Theology Discussion

Overview

This evening provides an opportunity to discuss theology and the teachings of the faith. A text is selected from Church documents or the writings of a theologian or saint. Then the text is distributed and discussed in small groups, with the help of some prepared questions.

Content

The theology discussion is a balance of two objectives: the communication of information, and the discussion of that information. In practice, what seems to work best is to take two or three paragraphs from a text, and then discuss them with prepared questions. The text could be drawn from anything of theological interest. It is helpful to keep in mind that the purpose of this evening is not so much to help people learn "facts" about theology, but to provide a context where people can reflect together on the gift of faith and assist each other to deepen their understanding.

Selection of the theme

Groups can approach the theology discussion in different ways. The core team should discuss the different possibilities and then, after agreeing on a particular approach, delegate the theology discussion evening to a coordinator and/or committee. The format for the theology discussion may vary from month to month, or it can follow a set theme for a certain number of months. In any case, the core team should review the format periodically, and discuss whether it needs to be tweaked or altered to meet the needs of the ministry.

Some ideas for selecting discussion topics:

- ▶ Select a number of topics, find appropriate texts, and prepare discussion questions.

- ▶ Take a section of a book and work through it from month to month.

- ▶ Take a theme (*e.g.*, the Holy Spirit) and pick different texts related to that theme for a period of months.

- ▶ Take a text from the *Catechism of the Catholic Church* relevant to the liturgical season or upcoming liturgical feast days.

Preparing the materials and the discussion questions

The materials and questions are best prepared by somebody with good theological knowledge. If the coordinator does not have special knowledge of theology or does not know where to start, one of the easiest things to do is simply to choose a section of the Catechism and work through it from month to month.

The questions should prompt two kinds of theological reflection. First, some questions should prompt reflection on what the text is saying about God, Jesus, the Church, and our destiny in Christ. Second, some questions should prompt reflection on the practical implications of the text in daily life. It helps to begin with some general questions, *e.g.*, "What are your initial thoughts on this passage?" or "Is there anything in particular about this text that strikes you or that makes you think?" Then one may proceed to more specific questions about what the text is saying, and then finally move to questions about how these theological ideas have application in daily life.

Week Five: Open Format

Overview

Any of the four standard formats can be used for a fifth monthly meeting. Since fifth monthly meetings happen only sporadically, they also provide an occasion to try something new or different.

Suggestions

The following are some suggestions for a fifth meeting:

▶ Movie night

▶ Social event

▶ Extended icebreakers, where a series of questions, some silly and some serious, are asked in the large group for the entire time of the meeting.

▶ Each participant is encouraged to bring a brief text with some spiritual significance (a Scripture text, a saint's writings, a poem, *etc.*) and read it for the group.

▶ A presentation and/or discussion about the life of a saint or blessed

▶ Charismatic prayer or healing service

▶ Extended praise and worship

▶ Mass of the day

Members should be encouraged to propose suggestions to the core team for fifth monthly meetings, especially if they would be willing to organize it.

The conclusion of the faith discussion

After the faith discussion portion of the meeting, everyone assembles together in one body. The ministry coordinator first invites people to make any announcements they might have, usually about other events and activities that are going on. The announcements are an important part of the evening. They explicitly connect the weekly meeting to the other activities of the ministry, and they also give newcomers a sense of what else is going on. After the announcements have concluded, the ministry coordinator leads everyone in a brief prayer, concluding with a common prayer such as an *"Our Father"* or a *"Hail Mary."*

Social gathering

The final phase of the evening—some kind of social gathering—is essential to the weekly meeting. The most typical thing is to head off to a restaurant/bar/coffeehouse.

If there is space in the parish center, from time to time it is good to organize gatherings at the parish center with refreshments instead of going out.

Chapter 4

Other Meetings and Activities

Overview

The purpose of the 20s/30s ministry is to create a Christ-centered community of young adults. Therefore, like any authentic community, it requires a variety of meetings and events in order to flourish. The weekly meeting provides an anchor, but it is only one aspect of the 20s/30s ministry. Other meetings and events are necessary to foster friendship, to reach out to young adults who would not feel comfortable coming to the weekly meeting (at least at first), and to orient the ministry toward direct service to others, especially the poor.

Besides the regular weekly meeting, the 20s/30s ministry should ideally organize other regular meetings and regular service opportunities. It is also beneficial to organize other one-time events that are social, service, and/or spiritual.

This chapter outlines various regular meetings and events that a 20s/30s ministry might want to consider organizing. The specifics of a particular 20s/30s ministry will determine which are most appropriate for a particular community. In all things, the core team should decide together which ideas to pursue, bearing in mind the need to add new activities organically, and also the need to ensure that the core team members are not overloaded.

Monthly Sunday Mass followed by brunch or dinner

Overview

Once a month, say on the 1st or 3rd Sunday, young adults are invited to attend a particular Sunday Mass, and then they head off to a restaurant for brunch or dinner. Alternatively the meal could be hosted in someone's home. Evening Masses often work well since they tend to get a larger crowd of young adults anyway. Such a monthly gathering serves many purposes: it connects the ministry explicitly with Sunday Eucharist; it ensures that at least once a month young adults will see other young adults at the same Mass; and it provides a comfortable point of entry for newcomers.

Bible/Theology Study

Overview

The Bible/Theology Study offers a venue for those participants interested in learning more about either Scripture or theology. It meets in cycles for a few consecutive weeks on a particular topic, ideally in someone's home. Then there is a break and a new cycle of meetings begins.

Selection of topic and materials

First, those interested in organizing the Bible/Theology Study gather to discuss possible topics, which may concern either Scripture or theology. Various study guides are available, and some of them are multi-media. Any text may serve as the basis for a particular study cycle. After the topic and materials have been selected, those involved then determine a schedule of meetings, usually 3 to 6 consecutive weekly meetings. A volunteer usually offers his or her home for the duration of the study. Otherwise the study group can meet on parish grounds.

Structure of the meeting

The participants may want to begin with some form of prayer. The rosary is a convenient, simple prayer form that works well. It also allows people to arrive slightly late without being disruptive.

The structure of the meeting itself varies according to the topic and materials that have been chosen. For example, participants may read a

Scripture text, and then discuss the study materials. Or they may listen to a CD or watch a DVD, and then discuss it. Sometimes, especially for sensitive topics, it may be helpful to break into smaller gender-based discussion groups, and then rejoin the large group for a concluding discussion.

It is important to set a firm wrap-up time for the discussion, so that those who need to leave do not feel uncomfortable leaving when they need to leave.

Ideally, the host and/or those attending provide refreshments either before, during, or after the meeting.

Monthly Social Event

Overview

The 20s/30s ministry strives to create community and foster friendship, and this objective requires a variety of social events in different contexts. A social coordinator, ideally assisted by a committee, oversees the planning of at least one social event per month. Others within the ministry may end up organizing other spontaneous social events during the course of any given month, and hopefully they will, but the idea is that each month the 20s/30s ministry offers at least one "official" social event.

Planning and suggestions

The monthly event can be anything from a cookout to a baseball game to the social aspect of a spiritual gathering (*e.g.,* a reception or party that accompanies a special liturgy or Mass). Here are some ideas that have worked well:

- ▸ Game nights (including card games)
- ▸ Texas Hold 'Em poker tournament
- ▸ Paintball (or similar type activities)

- Corn maze
- Karaoke
- Beer-making or beer-tasting with monastic beer (*i.e.*, beer made by monks)
- July 4th cookout and fireworks
- Super Bowl Party
- Christmas or Epiphany Party with "white elephant" re-gifting gift exchange
- Movie night
- New members night—a social gathering especially for new members to help them feel more welcome
- Bowling
- Trip to the beach
- *Iron Chef*-style cook-off
- Semi-formal progressive dinner, charging more than needed for food to raise money for some charity

Service Outreach

Overview

For any Christian community, serving others is both a responsibility and a gift. The 20s/30s ministry is no exception. This work both fulfills Christ's teaching and provides an important source of spiritual vitality and joy that ultimately feeds back into the 20s/30s ministry. Sometimes a ministry's service and justice outreach will emerge organically, without planning; often its participants are already very engaged in various forms of service before they start attending meetings. Yet it is almost always helpful for ministries to give focused thought and attention to their service outreach.

It is important to recognize that service includes both works of mercy and works of justice. Mercy and justice are interconnected but distinct aspects of the Church's social mission in the world. Works of mercy aim to provide immediate relief and assistance to those in need. Works of justice look to long-term, systemic change that can impact the struggles of people and communities locally and globally. For instance, helping at a soup kitchen or shelter is a work of mercy, while working to change structures that keep people trapped in poverty is a form of social justice. Because they often have fewer personal commitments, more free time, and a great deal of energy, young adults can be especially effective in works of both mercy and justice. Anything that the leadership can do to facilitate the ministry's engagement with this important aspect of the Church's mission is highly encouraged. The United States Conference of Catholic Bishops have many resources to assist leaders in this area, including a webpage dedicated to Catholic Social Teaching: http://www.usccb.org/beliefs-and-teachings/what-we-believe/catholic-social-teaching/index.cfm.

Organizing the ministry's service outreach

In organizing the ministry's service outreach, the service coordinator and the service committee may first want to inquire to discover what forms of outreach are already going on, especially in the parish, but also in the diocese as a whole. Important needs may have already been iden-tified, and the parish or diocese might warmly welcome the assistance of young adults. In general, intergenerational collaboration is desirable. Such collaboration benefits both young adults and older parishioners. It gives young adults an opportunity to learn from older parishioners and become more grounded in the local church community. In the process, older parishioners become encouraged and inspired by the faith and energy of the young adults.

In deciding upon collective forms of service, whether works of mercy or justice, another consideration is the commitment and numbers required by a particular ministry. For example, if the group commits to providing meals at a homeless shelter once a month, then a certain number of people must show up or people will go hungry. Regular visits to nursing home residents, however, do not have disastrous consequences if people do not show up. It is helpful to weigh such factors along with the interests and availability of ministry participants.

Practically speaking, often the best way to organize the ministry's service outreach is through a combination of low-key, regular activities that attract fewer people, and periodic large-scale events on a quarterly basis that require and attract a larger number of people. This balance ensures that service outreach is a consistent aspect of the ministry's activities, without pushing participants beyond their availability and energy.

Individual forms of parish service can also be encouraged, such serving as Eucharistic ministers and lectors. This cultivates the ministry's connection with the concrete life of the parish. It also raises the ministry's visibility in the parish, which both draws other young adults to the parish and the ministry, and encourages older parishioners.

The USCCCB has developed a great resource about service, charity, and social justice called *Communities of Salt and Light*, which can be found at www.wearesaltandlight.org.

Some ideas for regular service outreach

The following are some suggestions for regular, low-key forms of service that could be organized as a form of collective outreach. Some of these are dependent on local circumstances. For example, on the Mexican border, there may be more opportunities to assist with immigration and migration issues, while in certain inner city neighborhoods, there may be more possibilities to connect with urban-specific poverty and homelessness.

- ▶ Visiting nursing home residents
- ▶ Some form of ministry to the homeless
  (*e.g.*, monthly preparation of sandwiches)

▶ Advocacy for the needs of a local ministry
(*e.g.*, immigrants, migrants, homeless)

▶ Writing to local government leaders on particular issues
important to Catholics

▶ Environmental service (*e.g.*, cleaning part of road,
maintaining public grounds)

▶ Contacting the diocese and making ministry participants
available to speak at schools and youth retreats about faith

▶ Participating in area pro-life prayer vigil or rosary walk

▶ Helping at a local ReStore (Habitat for Humanity resale
shops, available in certain areas)

▶ Teaching religious education classes in the parish in teams

▶ Volunteering with parish youth ministry

▶ Volunteering with area pregnancy center

Some ideas for one-time service events

The following are some suggestions for one-time service events, some of
which could be done annually:

▶ Volunteering to help with annual parish festival

▶ Housework or yardwork for elderly parishioner identified
by the pastor

▶ Day-long Habitat for Humanity project

▶ Singing Christmas carols at area nursing homes

▶ Spring or summer mission trip

▶ Participating in a peaceful protest stemming from our faith
and social commitments for a worthy cause

Sports and Outdoor Activities

Overview

Ideally the spectrum of the ministry's activities should include sports and outdoor activities. There are many advantages. They provide a natural outlet for the energy and interests of many 20/30-somethings. They also provide a non-threatening point of entry, especially for those who are non-Catholic, or who are Catholic but uncomfortable about participating in more explicitly religious meetings. Hiking and camping trips can be especially appropriate for 20s/30s ministry events, since they give young adults a chance to encounter the beauty of God's creation.

Sports

Some combination of regular and sporadic events can be ideal. Softball, kickball, ultimate Frisbee, volleyball, and similar sports are particularly suited to a 20s/30s ministry because men and women feel more comfortable playing such sports together, and because they do not require great skill. Runners and cyclists can also organize regular runs or cycling. The ministry may want to enter a team in a local sporting league. Whatever is done, it is important that the activity be regular and (ideally) weekly, so that people always know that there will be something going on at a certain time and place. Weekend afternoons work particularly well, and they lend themselves to impromptu social gatherings afterwards in the evening.

Outdoor activities

Outdoor activities require more planning, and therefore tend to be less regular. A combination of day trips and overnight trips generally works best, so that those less familiar with hiking and camping can ease their way into new experiences. White water rafting trips can work well too. The ministry may want to offer one big annual outing each summer, such as a weekend camping trip in a nearby state park.

Annual Retreat

Overview

Every year the ministry should ideally sponsor some kind of annual retreat. There are a variety of formats that can be chosen. Depending on its needs and resources, the ministry may want to design its own retreat, or attend something offered by a monastery or retreat center.

Planning the retreat

There are many possible approaches to an annual retreat. The first step is to decide whether to attend a retreat offered by another church community, or to plan a retreat specifically for the group. There are advantages to each approach: the former connects the ministry to others, and the latter builds internal community spirit. Then the actual format of the retreat itself and its location should be decided. The chaplain and/ or the advisor should be involved in these discussions, as they may well have many insights and suggestions, especially if they will be expected to play a special role in the actual retreat. The winter is often a good time to schedule a retreat, because there is not as much competition with other event planning.

Resources

Some resources deserve special note.

▶ *Charis Ministries*, based in Chicago, has developed a retreat program based on Ignatian spirituality particularly for young adults. It organizes retreats and also offers planning materials for those organizing their own retreats. A similar outreach, Christus Ministries, based in California, is another alternative for retreat ministry. See http://charis.website and http://www.christusministries.org.

▶ *Hearts on Fire*, based in Milwaukee, has also developed a retreat program for young adults based on Ignatian spirituality. See http://apostleshipofprayer.org/hearts-on-fire.

> *Local monasteries* are a great resource for retreats. Many are particularly geared to hosting retreatants and may be able accommodate a young adult retreat. A simple weekend schedule that involves joining the monastic community for prayers and Mass, perhaps supplemented with time for *lectio divina*, rosary, and/or Eucharistic adoration, can provide the backbone of a low-maintenance but nonetheless spiritually graced weekend. One of the monks or nuns may be available to give two or three talks, and perhaps with time for group discussion and a social gathering on Saturday night, a full and satisfying weekend is fairly easy to plan.

Young Adult Conferences

Young adult conferences, when available, provide an important avenue to connect with the wider young adult community (or to a specific category of young adults, such as singles or couples). Dioceses and other national organizations or apostolates sometimes sponsor young adult conferences for a day or weekend. They may also be called "days of reflection." If the local diocese or any nearby organization or apostolate does not offer something like this, the diocesan young adult ministry office might be able to suggest a nearby diocese or organization that does. In some instances, such as in Southern California, there may be a young adult component to a larger Catholic event or conference (in that case, the Los Angeles Religious Education Congress). Either way, such conferences provide excellent opportunities for young adults to have an experience of the universal Church.

World Youth Day

The international World Youth Day pilgrimage is aimed primarily at young adults (the age range recommended by the USCCB for that gathering is 16 to 35), so this is yet another opportunity for the 20s/30s ministry to connect with the experience of the universal Church. For those who have the means to travel, the international event is held every three years in different countries around the world. Young adults from every country and walk of life have found these pilgrimages inspirational and transformative. They provide a unique experience of the universality of the Catholic Church. They also provide an opportunity to meet other young adults, to listen to theological and catechetical presentations, and to meet the Holy Father in person. They can also be a great bonding experience for a particular 20s/ 30s ministry. For young adults who cannot travel to the international World Youth Day, the USCCB encourages the development of "stateside" at-home celebrations of this pilgrimage, bringing together youth and young adults in a diocese or region for a similar experience of faith. These experiences also provide a great opportunity for local 20s/30s ministries. For more information about these opportunities, go to www.wydusa.org.

Other Spiritual Events

Overview

Periodic spiritual events, often tied to the church's liturgical year, contribute in significant ways to the life of the 20s/30s ministry. They are often most successful when combined with a social element.

Some ideas and suggestions

Here are some suggestions for occasional or annual events of a spiritual nature.

- ▶ Opportunity for confession during weekly meeting's adoration or prayer two to four times per year (including Advent and Lent)

- ▶ Occasional Mass during a weekly 20s/30s meeting, either instead of adoration or prayer, or immediately afterwards

- ▶ New Year's Eve Midnight Mass, perhaps preceded by some time for Eucharistic adoration beforehand. It can be preceded or followed by a party, either at a participant's house, or at the parish center.

▶ Attendance as a ministry at local Theology on Tap gatherings (or similar programs), perhaps cancelling normal weekly meetings if they are on the same night as that event. Attendance at Theology on Tap is a great way to network with other young adults.

▶ Especially for young adult couples (dating, engaged, or married): a special Mass and dinner for couples (with music, dancing, or entertainment), perhaps around Valentine's Day (Feb. 14) or during the summer months (when many married couples celebrate their anniversaries). Such events provide a great way to engage young adult couples in the community and affirm the Sacrament of Marriage and the primacy of the family. The Mass can include a renewal of vows for the married couples in attendance, or a special blessing for engaged couples in preparation for their wedding.

▶ Vigil of the Saints on October 31: This liturgy involves readings from saints or saints' biographies in a darkened church, followed by a homily, Night Prayer and a candle-lit procession and chanting of a Litany of Saints. Afterwards there is a reception. This liturgy was developed in Washington, DC, at the Dominican House of Studies, where it is particularly popular with young adults.

▶ Extended Pentecost Vigil Celebration: For the early Christians, the Vigil of Pentecost was one of the most important celebrations of the year. There is still an extended version of the Vigil Mass "on the books" that is rarely used, dedicated to praying for a new outpouring of the Holy Spirit. The positive theme of hope and renewal and new life is a natural fit for a young adult ministry, and a day-long celebration can be built around the Pentecost Vigil Mass. In the afternoon, there can be outdoor games, small group faith discussions, a grill-out, and then some time of prayer before Mass. The prayer before Mass can include Eucharistic adoration, First Vespers of Pentecost, praying of the third glorious mystery of the rosary (*i.e.*, the descent of the Holy Spirit on Pentecost), and opportunity for confession. The readings and prayers for the extended vigil of Pentecost are available in liturgical books. After the Mass, there can be a party. The celebration can also provides a natural occasion to host a meeting of representatives from different area young adult ministries, to network and exchange ideas on connecting with and ministering to young adults in the wider community. See www.pentecost20s30s.com for more information.

▶ Pilgrimage Road Trip: International pilgrimages are a great experience for a ministry, but they can be too expensive or time-consuming for young adults. There are a number of places, however, that are easily accessible by car within the United States. Carpooling and camping can significantly minimize expenses. In the U.S., among the many possibilities, there are notable shrines dedicated to the North American Martyrs and St. Kateri Tekakwitha (in Auriesville and Fonda, NY), St. Elizabeth Ann Seton (in Emmitsburg, MD), St. John Paul II and the Immaculate Conception, plus a Franciscan Monastery with reconstructions of key sites in the Holy Land (all in Washington, DC), the Passion of Christ (in St. John, IN), the Spanish missions (near San Antonio, TX, and across California), and the oldest Catholic parish in the United States (in St. Augustine, FL). In Canada, there are also many great options, including the martyrs' shrine in Midland, Ontario, and many shrines in Montreal, Trois-Rivieres, and Quebec City. In Mexico there is the shrine of Our Lady of Guadalupe. There are also many other lesser-known shrines or monasteries in different parts of the country that could serve as the focal point of a road trip pilgrimage.

▶ Ecumenical or interreligious activities: perhaps partnering or gathering with young adults from a nearby Christian church (for ecumenical programming) or a Jewish synagogue, Muslim mosque, Hindu temple, or other religious center in the community. Young adults could also take a tour and/or hear about the spirituality or religious practices of that denomination or religion from the local pastor or faith leader.

Other ideas for regular meetings and activities

Overview

The ministry should make it clear that anybody who wants to start a new activity is always welcome to give it a try. Such ideas should be first discussed at a core team meeting to make sure there is consensus and so that the core team's feedback can be incorporated. Nonetheless, the presumption would be that, unless there would be a direct conflict with some other dimension of the ministry's activities, those who have the energy and inspiration for something new should be encouraged to try and get something going.

Suggestions

▶ Book club where participants meet to discuss books or novels of whatever sort, religious or non-religious

▶ Intercessory prayer ministry where participants are part of an email ministry and pray for petitions sent to the ministry; the ministry may also meet to pray together

▶ Charismatic prayer group

▶ Women's group

▶ Men's group

▶ Foreign movie club where participants watch foreign movies and discuss them

Chapter 5

Going to the Margins

Overview

Soon after his election, in June 2013, Pope Francis told the people of Rome: "All the peripheries, all the crossroads on the way: go there. And sow there the seed of the Gospel with your words and your witness." Going to the margins is central to Christian discipleship. Jesus compares the kingdom of God to a king who sends servants into the streets to invite everyone they can find to a wedding feast (Matt 22:9). Then, before ascending to the Father, Jesus commissions his disciples to fulfill the parable by inviting everyone they can find to the Eucharistic banquet: "Go into the whole world and proclaim the gospel to every creature" (Mark 16:15)." This commission applies also to every 20s/30s ministry. Living out this commission requires not only careful thought and planning, but also compassionate sensitivity to the pastoral needs of those living on the peripheries of society and the Church.

Reaching young adults who are not active in the Church (whether raised Catholic or not) and bringing them God's message of love and mercy is one of the most urgent priorities of the Catholic Church in the United States and around the world. Yet the sheer desire to invite young adults into the life of the Church is not enough. Finding effective ways to communicate the Gospel and the attractiveness of Christian community requires prayerful reflection, compassionate listening, and prudent allocation of energy and resources. It is necessary, therefore, for each 20s/30s ministry and especially its leadership to give regular attention to how it can better serve young adults who are not yet active in the life of the Church.

Pastoral vision

The Second Vatican Council emphasized that the entire People of God share in Christ's prophetic ministry and thus share in the task of evangelization. Young adults active in the practice of their faith are themselves the most crucial means to reaching inactive or less active young adults. No pastoral program, no matter how well designed, can suffice on its own to reach them and draw them into the life of the Church. Only the encounter with Christ mediated by his disciples and the Holy Spirit has any chance of real success. As Pope Benedict wrote, "Being Christian is not the result of an ethical choice or a lofty idea, but the encounter with an event, a person, which gives life a new horizon and a decisive direction" (*Deus Caritas Est*, 1).

Paradoxically, the first step to going to the margins is building up the center. Unless the 20s/30s ministry first succeeds in establishing a vibrant community, it will have nothing to invite inactive or less active young adults to be part of. What inactive young adult would want to come to a Church-sponsored gathering for inactive young adults? Indifferent or disaffected young adults might come once to air their concerns, but they would not come a second time. They would have no reason to return. Furthermore, going to the margins—if it is truly going to the margins—is often challenging and energy-depleting. If participants in the ministry are not being nourished and strengthened in their faith, they will not have the spiritual energy or spontaneous joy necessary for effective outreach.

A planetary analogy can be helpful. The heart of every 20s/30s ministry is provided by those young adults most committed to the ministry. Especially through the weekly meetings, these young adults and their friendships with each other provide a gravitational core around which the rest of the ministry orbits. Without this gravitational core, less active or less committed young adults would not be attracted to the ministry; it gives the ministry spark and energy. By the same token, the success of the ministry in reaching inactive young adults depends on having a flourishing community of Catholic young adults deeply committed to their faith.

Yet as important as it is to establish a community to which inactive or less active young adults can be invited, it is not enough. The 20s/30s ministry must also actively seek them out and invite them to be part of its community. Care should be taken to welcome all young adults to the ministry, not just those who regularly attend Mass at the parish or those who are already active in their faith and have time for additional activities in the community.

With this in mind, leaders should be conscious of looking to the margins to see who is not there, that is, those who do not normally attend ministry events and activities. Building a young adult ministry with these people in mind will be very important. Some of these men and women on the margins might include:

- ▶ Those who attend church semi-regularly (perhaps once per month, or only a few times per year), but who are spiritually open.

- ▶ Those who might attend church regularly, but because of time constraints (multiple jobs or jobs with challenging hours; family responsibilities; pressures and expectations from work, family, or society; financial difficulty; distance from parish; or other limiting factors), are not able to be involved elsewhere.

- ▶ Those who are hurting, whether struggling with economic hardship, debt, long hours, medical issues, psychological trauma, mental health, family pressure; overwhelmed by expectations, guilt, or addiction; or uncertain about their life or their faith.

- ▶ Those who live in poverty, are unemployed or underemployed.

- ▶ Those who face challenges related to relationships or sexuality.

- ▶ Those who consider themselves "spiritual but not religious," or who might be skeptical or uncertain about the Church.

- ▶ Those who feel rejected by or alienated from the Church, due to past pains or questions about the faith.

- ▸ Those who feel detached from the parish due to racial or cultural anxieties, or a feeling of being unwelcome due to their race, culture, or language.

- ▸ Those who are active in the parish or diocese, but who have already committed to other ministries (liturgical ministries, charity and justice work, youth or children's ministries, etc.) or volunteer work in the community.

While a 20s/30s ministry does not need to include every one of these groups, it is important that leaders be aware of looking beyond the regular participants and those who have the time, freedom, or economic ability to be involved in such activities. Experience has shown again and again that Christian communities thrive especially when they are generous in reaching out the marginalized and excluded. Not only does their generosity itself multiply the community's joy, but those who end up being drawn to the community often bring new life, new energy, and a special kind of joy. By the same token, young adult ministries can often fall apart if they remain homogenous or limited in their invitational scope.

Practical steps

After identifying particular subgroups of young adults that they want to serve better, ministries should feel great freedom in experimenting with different ideas and different strategies, and also freedom to fail: the important thing is to try; success is often beyond our control. Practical steps for reaching inactive or less active young adults include:

- ▸ Make events and activities with less explicitly religious elements part of the ministry's regular programming

- ▸ Encourage participants to invite their friends to ministry activities

- ▸ Hold periodic gatherings in a participant's home specifically to welcome newcomers to the ministry

▶ Hold weekly gatherings (or least monthly or bimonthly gatherings) in a secular setting: restaurant, community or social center, library, etc.

▶ Develop publicity and promotion with inactive young adults especially in mind

▶ Have the core team regularly evaluate:

• whether the ministry's activities and programming are sufficiently attractive to those on the margins

• whether the expense of programming options is frequently cost-prohibitive to young adults with less financial means, or whether financial support can be made available (for example, by arranging for anonymous support to attend weekend retreats, perhaps mediated through the parish priest)

• whether the scheduling of programming options excludes segments of the community, and whether key activities or events should be rescheduled

▶ Connect with diocesan or local ministries focused on cultural diversity and either (a) work with them to reach young people of cultural families outside of the dominant cultural family of the parish or region or (b) draw on their resources and suggestions to develop a new outreach

▶ Have the core team actively participate in training for intercultural outreach

▶ Develop programming for the 20s/30s ministry focused on the needs of those going through economic, cultural, family, or health struggles, such as small group sessions on the topics of stress at work, family disagreements, or financial uncertainty

- ▸ Engage young adults and find ways to invite them to either parish activities or the 20s/30s ministry during "moments of return": specifically, Christmas, Ash Wednesday, Holy Week and Easter, and weddings and baptisms

- ▸ Ensuring that the 20s/30s ministry is present to young adults in times of grief (funerals, national or international crises, sickness, etc.)

- ▸ Host programming or activities drawing on Catholic spiritualities (Franciscan, Ignatian, Dominican, Benedictine, etc.) and/or various forms of prayer (Taize, contemplative, imaginative, liturgy of the hours, etc.) that might hold special appeal to those who consider themselves "spiritual but not religious."

- ▸ Host a big annual event, especially geared to attracting newcomers, such as an extended Pentecost Vigil celebration (see Chapter 4 and www.pentecost20s30s.com)

Chapter 6

Choosing An Age Range

Overview

The choice of age range is one of the most important decisions a 20s/30 ministry will make. As mentioned earlier, the United States Conference of Catholic Bishops' pastoral plan for young adult ministry, *Sons and Daughters of the Light* (1996), describes young adulthood as encompassing a broad age spectrum: men and women in their late teens, twenties, and thirties.

20s/30s ministries may want to include everyone who fits that demographic, or they may want to focus on a particular age bracket. They may also want to develop sub-groups according to age span within a larger ministry. There are pros and cons to every possible option. When founding a new ministry, organizers should give this question special attention. This chapter discusses the principle options and their pros and cons.

The 20s Ministry (20–29)

20s ministries are especially effective in ministering to the particular needs of 20-something Catholics. The reason is simple: 20-somethings generally prefer to socialize with other 20-somethings, especially if they are looking for a spouse. This preference is understandable. People in their 20s are at a very different stage of life than people in their 30s. Experience shows that when 20-somethings show up to young adult meetings and find that most participants are in their 30s, they are unlikely to return. Yet unless young adult ministries are especially large and diverse, they tend to drift older and older. Eventually, most participants end up in their 30s. Once that happens, the ministry will no longer be able to attract young adults in their 20s. For these reasons, some ministries may want to adopt an age range of 20-29, or perhaps 18-32.

The downside of excluding 30-somethings is significant and should be weighed carefully. Yet not every ministry is meant to serve everyone. For example, women's groups exclude men, but they could not accomplish their mission if they did not. Likewise, some young adult ministries may need to focus on 20-somethings to accomplish their mission.

If a ministry decides to focus on young adults in their 20s, two important practical points are advisable. First, it is helpful to put the words "20s ministry" in the ministry's official name. Doing so clearly defines the ministry's age range. It helps people avoid the awkward situation of showing up to a ministry and finding out that they are not the right age. It also makes it easier to maintain the ministry's intended age demographic. (It is helpful to keep in mind that people often think that "young adult ministries" are for teenagers. Even those familiar with church lingo often need to check a young adult ministry's materials to see which age demographic it serves.) Second, ministry coordinators should maintain awareness of other, older young adult ministries in the area, so that older young adults can be referred to them. It may also want to think ahead and create spin-off 30s ministries to accommodate former participants who have aged-out.

The Early 20s Ministry (20–25 or 18–25)

Another way to minister to 20-somethings is to focus on young adults age 20-25. Such ministries can be especially effective when ministering to an overlapping combination of college students and working young adults in urban settings.

The Mid-Range Young Adult Ministry (20–35)

This age range is more inclusive than a 20s ministry. In many ways, it is the best of both worlds. By welcoming participants up to the age of 35, more Catholic young adults can participate, and yet, because its age range is tilted toward the 20s, it keeps the average age of the ministry down and more easily attracts younger participants.

This sort of age range, however, is not easily put in the ministry's name, because calling it "The St. X 20-35 Ministry" sounds awkward. As a result, it is difficult to publicize or maintain.

The Full 20s/30s Ministry (20–39)

The advantage of this age range is that it is extremely inclusive. The disadvantage is that ministries with this age range tend to drift older and older, to the point that they eventually include only people 30 and over. If this age range is used, it is helpful to have "20s/30s" in the ministry's name. Such a name makes the ministry's identity clear.

The 30s Ministry (30–39) / The 30s+ Ministry (30+)

These age ranges allow older young adults to socialize among their peers. However, it should be said that it is not clear whether the model given in this guide is a good fit for these age demographics. The 20s/30s model requires a great deal of energy and enthusiasm. Young adults past their early 30s tend to be in a different state of mind. They have matured and are more established, and their interests are different. Consequently, the model proposed here may not work as well with an older age range. Experience also shows that ministries focused on 30-somethings tend to attract fewer participants than 20s ministries or 20s/30s ministries.

Adjusting the age range

For additional flexibility, in its official materials, the ministry may want to state explicitly that it welcomes young adults slightly younger or slightly older than its age range. For example, a 20s ministry may want to state that its age range extends from 18–32. This approach allows for greater inclusivity (with a special outreach to those young adults of traditional college-age). It also allows for young adults to age out of the ministry gradually, rather than discontinuing their participation on the day of their birthday. Whatever is decided, the ministry's official materials should state its policy clearly.

Discerning between the options

Often the most important consideration when discerning between the different options is an obvious one: what are the ages of the young adults trying to get the ministry started? If they are all recent college graduates, then they may want to start a 20s ministry. If they are a mix of ages, then they will probably want to choose a more expansive age demographic. Another consideration is population density. In areas with lower populations, it may be necessary to broaden the age range in order to attract a sufficient number of young adults to create a viable and vibrant group. Whatever options they consider, the ministry founders should feel great freedom to select any age range that seems right to them. Their job is not to do everything, but to discern the best way forward for their ministry in a particular time and place and cultural context.

Chapter 7

Communication, Publicity and Networking

Overview

Communication, publicity and networking are essential elements of a thriving 20s/30s ministry. This chapter offers some suggestions for internal and external communication.

Website and social media

Every 20s/30s ministry needs its own website or webpage, or at least a social media page, such as Facebook or Twitter. The parish may have space for the ministry on the general parish website, or it may be necessary to acquire a new domain. The website and social media pages are important points of reference for the ministry, especially when it comes to attracting new participants. It is helpful if the website and social media pages are updated frequently, *e.g.*, with pictures, upcoming events, *etc.* The website and social media pages can also be a convenient place to make flyers or other resources available for download.

Ministry emails

Unless some form of social media is used instead (such as tweets), email is a very important form of communication within the ministry. Some sites and email providers offer free ministry services that allow participants to email the entire ministry without having to enter individual emails. The ministry should create two ministry email lists, one for the ministry at large and one for the core team, or else something comparable through social media.

Weekly emails

Every week, the ministry coordinator or somebody delegated should send out an email (or other communication) to the ministry with information about that week's main meeting, along with any other meetings and events going on that week or in the near future. Ministry participants can also send other announcements to the coordinator to be included in this weekly communication.

Those responsible for certain meetings and events—such as the weekly Bible Study or a game of ultimate Frisbee—may want to send out reminder emails or social media notifications with more detailed information.

Ministry policy for email and social media

Generally, it works best to allow everybody to communicate the ministry directly, rather than have every email or notification first cleared by someone in charge of the email list. For instance, somebody might want to organize a social gathering or a movie at the last minute. Similarly, somebody might want to send out something inspirational or humorous.

From time to time, people may cause problems with inappropriate or overly frequent emails. In most cases, these problems can be addressed by simply taking it up with the individual, but if necessary the core team may want to restrict an individual's ability to email to the ministry. Generally speaking, it is good to ask participants not to raise controversial issues using email lists or social media. Individual ministries may want to lay down other ground rules for the emails. Some young adults may prefer not to receive frequent emails, and most email services allow users to limit the amount of emails they receive (*e.g.*, they can request through the email service to receive fewer emails, so that all of the emails sent out in a given day or week are compiled into one email).

Participant list

It is a good idea to compile a list of participants' addresses and phone numbers so that they can be reached directly. The list can then be made available to other ministry participants. Participants should always be asked, however, whether they want to share their personal information with the rest of the ministry.

Getting the word out

To thrive, ministries need to dedicate conscious effort to getting the word out. The rule "the more the merrier" applies especially to young adults. A steady stream of new participants brings freshness and vitality. It also ensures that there are new faces to replace those who drop out or move away.

Beyond these obvious considerations, an orientation toward attracting and welcoming new participants has a subtle but very important effect on the atmosphere of the ministry. Having such a focus prevents the ministry from forming cliques and turning inward. People naturally start thinking in terms of welcoming newcomers, and being open to others rather than just their own needs.

In the end, however, the best way to attract new participants is to make sure the ministry's activities are running smoothly and people are having a good time. Even without being encouraged to do so, if the ministry is thriving, people will naturally invite friends, because they are having such a good time, and they want others to experience it, too.

Parish bulletins

The 20s/30s ministry should put frequent announcements in the parish bulletin. Although many young adults do not read the bulletin, parents and relatives may notice something, and then encourage young adults they know to attend. It is also encouraging for parishioners to see that young adults are doing something in the parish. Announcements can also be sent to neighboring parishes for their bulletins, at least periodically if those parishes do not have their own young adult ministries.

Pulpit announcements

One of the most effective ways to attract new participants is to have participants make brief announcements during Mass, and then stay around afterwards to talk to parishioners. Even if there are not many young adults at a particular Mass, someone attending might know young adults and then tell them about it. Ministry participants may also want to inquire with pastors at neighboring parishes and ask to speak in their parishes as well. It can be especially effective to time pulpit announcements with an upcoming special event (*e.g.*, a volleyball game or a cook-out).

Networking

Connecting with other parishes

The 20s/30s ministry may find that other area parishes are very interested in supporting its ministry. Many parishes may not have the resources to support their own young adult ministry, but would be happy to publicize what is going on in a nearby parish.

Connecting with campus ministries

It can be very helpful for the 20s/30s ministry to connect with local campus ministries. Such connections attract new participants, and the witness of young adults living their faith can be encouraging and inspiring to college students, and give them a vision of life after college. It also may inspire out-of-state college students to establish a 20s/30s ministry in their home parishes after they graduate.

Connecting with the diocese

It is very important for a 20s/30s ministry to connect with the person(s) in charge of young adult ministry for the diocese. The diocese may be able to provide helpful guidance, suggestions, and resources. It may also have a list of young adult ministries which can be useful for networking.

Connecting with other ministries

Young adults enjoy meeting new people and connecting with other ministries besides their own. These sorts of connections can be fostered in a number of different ways. Multiple ministries can co-sponsor the same event (such as a Theology on Tap series), join in the same trip, attend the same young adult conference together, *etc.* They may also want to send representatives of their respective leadership teams to meet and discuss how they go about things, and what works and what doesn't, and in this way exchange ideas and encourage each other. But regardless of what form collaboration might take, the key thing is to open the lines of communication and develop friendships and relationships. The rest will happen naturally and organically.

Chapter 8

Starting a 20s/30s Ministry

Overview

The guide thus far has given a vision of what a fully established 20s/30s ministry might look like. Starting a 20s/30s ministry from scratch is complex and challenging, and it requires flexibility and a willingness to try things that might not work. Moreover, the model presented in this guide may not be appropriate for every situation. This chapter makes some suggestions for how to go about starting a 20s/30s ministry, and how to adapt this model of ministry to particular circumstances. These suggestions should be seen for what they are—suggestions—and each ministry should experiment and try what seems right to them.

Pray!

The first and most important step is to pray for God's help and the guidance of the Holy Spirit. And don't just pray, ask other people to pray. If there are local religious communities, call them up and ask them to pray for this intention. Ask pastors to see if there are ways that this intention can be incorporated into the prayers of the parish. Parishioners may be interested in gathering for a special time of prayer for young adults: older parishioners are often concerned about the spiritual well-being of younger Catholics and may be very pleased to be asked to pray for this intention. It may also be possible to add petitions to the intercessions during Sunday Mass. Christ assures us that this prayer will bear fruit: "Amen, I say to you, if two of you agree on earth about anything for which they are to pray, it shall be granted to them by my heavenly Father." (Mt 18:19) He also guarantees that the Holy Spirit will be given to all who ask: "If you then, who are wicked, know how to give good gifts to your children, how much more will the Father in heaven give the holy Spirit to those who ask him?" (Lk 11:13) Any time given to prayer for God's help in the founding of a 20s/30s ministry will always prove well worth it.

Concrete steps

Find a home-base parish

Find a parish to sponsor and support the 20s/30s ministry. The availability for this ministry of a priest, deacon, or pastoral associate is an important consideration, but not absolutely necessary. Other important considerations include the meeting facilities of the parish and the concentration of young adults living in the parish or nearby environs.

Multiple parishes working together as a team may want to sponsor a single 20s/30s ministry. Still, it is advisable to have the main weekly meeting at the same parish every week. It avoids confusion about where the ministry is meeting any given week. It also grounds the ministry more concretely in the life of the Church. It helps the ministry to see itself as part of parish life, and not just using space at different churches. It can be beneficial for other sponsoring parishes to host other events and regular meetings, however. (For more on the topic of regional 20s/30s ministries, see Chapter 8.)

Find interested young adults

Find a core group of young adults interested in starting a 20s/30s ministry. Ten seems to be a good threshold number. (It also constitutes a *minyan*, the minimum number traditionally required for Jewish public prayer.) If there are fewer than ten young adults who are nonetheless committed to making something happen, the best way forward may be to pray together for this intention, perhaps during times of Eucharistic adoration, and to spend time together getting to know each other better, perhaps with faith discussions of one kind or another—and then just wait to see if God ends up sending other people their way. If the core group remains smaller than ten, then it might be better to try something else, perhaps a small informal bible study. Alternatively, the core group could together attend an existing parish ministry that is not exclusively for young adults but nonetheless seems appropriate and beneficial.

If the organizers find it difficult to gather an initial core group of young adults, they may want to coordinate a gathering of interested young adults after moments in the liturgical year when young adults tend to return to active participation in parish life, such as Ash Wednesday, Palm Sunday, or Easter, or when college students or recent college graduates return to the area. The parish youth minister may be able to help identify alum of the youth ministry program who would be interested in being part of a 20s/30s ministry.

Hold an organizational meeting

Before holding any formal meetings, hold an organizational meeting, and advertise it through parish bulletins, pulpit announcements, diocesan newsletters, *etc.*, and ask those young adults who have already expressed interest to invite their friends.

At this meeting, a brief vision of what a 20s/30s ministry is about should be presented and discussed. After a brief discussion, those present should try to move toward a consensus about how to proceed. The ministry may want to have a special gathering to kick off the ministry's establishment—perhaps a cookout or a special Mass and dinner—or it may simply want to begin with the standard weekly meeting. In any case, at this organizational meeting, it will be important to set a night and a time for the regular weekly meeting. Various individuals will need to take responsibility for preparing whatever is decided.

One of the most important decisions to make at this organizational meeting is the age range of the ministry. Will it be 20–29, 20–35, 20–39, or something else entirely? Each age bracket has different pros and cons (as discussed in Chapter 5). Deciding this question should be one of the first orders of business.

Establish the core team

Extend an open invitation to join the initial core team. Volunteers may be requested before, after, or during the initial organizational meeting. Volunteers should be asked to commit to a set period of time, something like six months. There may be rough spots as the ministry gets started, but after six months, the core team should have a good sense of whether or not the ministry will be able to sustain itself. It may be that it can't, in which case there is no harm in acknowledging that fact, and perhaps disbanding or trying something else.

Until the ministry has time to settle down and get its bearings, it may best for people to volunteer for different organizational responsibilities on an *ad hoc* basis, without assigning distinct roles. Or people may prefer to take on positions right from the beginning. In any case, once the core team feels like things have settled sufficiently, or as soon as growing numbers make it necessary, a ministry coordinator should be appointed for one year, and other core team positions likewise taken up for one year.

Discuss and put in writing descriptions of the ministry's mission, the core team's organization, and basic ministry policies

The core team should discuss and put in writing the ministry's purpose, organization, and policies. Such discussions will clarify the nature and purpose of the ministry, heighten the core team's sense of ownership, and prevent miscommunication. It is important that the core team's decisions be put into writing for future reference. They should also be made available to the rest of the ministry. Much of it, but perhaps not all, should be posted on the ministry's website.

The best timing for such discussions varies. Some may want to figure things out from the very beginning. Others may want to operate according to provisional guidelines, and address these issues only after the ministry has come into its own rhythm. In either case, the core team may find it helpful to conduct these discussions in the context of a planning retreat.

Begin the weekly meeting

The most important element to get started is the weekly meeting. It may be the case that there are no musicians able to provide contemporary music during adoration. If so, the ministry should decide whether to meet for quiet adoration or wait until a musician can be recruited. For the faith discussion portion of the evening, the ministry may want to use only those formats that it finds easier to prepare (*e.g.*, the Scripture format). Once things have settled down, and more volunteers come forward to help with the preparation work, other formats can be added to the rotation.

Advertise widely

Once the ministry has started to meet regularly, it is important to flood all relevant channels with publicity and advertisements (see Chapter 6 for more suggestions). In this beginning stage, it is important to build up a critical mass of young adults as soon as possible. Ask ministry participants to spread the word with family and friends.

As when identifying an initial core group of young adults, young adult moments of return—times when young adults often return to active participation in parish life—are good opportunities to promote special events and the 20s/30s ministry in general. Particularly appropriate opportunities include: during Lent, especially around Ash Wednesday and Palm Sunday, at Christmas and Easter, times when college students and recent college graduates reconnect with their youth ministry, marriage and baptismal preparation (and at weddings and baptisms). In general, when seeking opportunities to promote and advertise the 20s/30s ministry, look for those times when young adults are more likely to revisit the parish community.

Gradually add other elements

As things grow and develop, the core team will naturally want to expand the activities of the ministry or refine how it goes about things. It is best to let this happen organically, without rushing or forcing things and thus overburdening core team members. Hopefully as the ministry grows, the core team will as well, and this will provide new volunteers to organize new events without overworking any particular individual. In the initial stages of establishing a 20s/30s ministry, rather than focusing on adding activities as quickly as possible, it is much more important for the core team to make special effort to proceed by consensus and guard internal unity, so that everybody feels good about how things are progressing.

Chapter 9

Regional 20s/30s Ministries and Diocesan Organizations

Overview

This chapter will discuss two separate issues: how to adopt the 20s/30s model for regional ministries, and how to set up regional and diocesan structures for organizing multiple 20s/30s ministries in the same diocese.

Regional 20s/30s Ministries

20s/30s ministries by their nature tend to attract young adults from multiple parishes. In certain circumstances, however, it may be preferable to have a regional ministry that is explicitly organized as the common project of multiple parishes, or perhaps a diocesan deanery.

It is easy for a regional cluster to incorporate the basic elements of the 20s/30s model. The question is how to go about dividing these elements among the different parishes and/or other Catholic institutions sponsoring this regional ministry. The central challenge is figuring out a way, in very particular circumstances, of how to involve multiple parishes in the regular activities of the 20s/30s ministry.

The most important decision is when and where to hold the main weekly meeting. The main weekly meeting is the anchor of the 20s/30s ministry model. As such, the vitality of the ministry depends greatly on its success. From the perspective of the core team, it is easier if it is at the same place every week, because it minimizes hassles in making the necessary day-to-day ordinary preparations for adoration, arranging the meeting space, *etc.*, and thus keeps the weekly meetings low-maintenance. From the perspective of the 20s/30s ministry at large, it is also better if it is held at the same place: the stability and regularity foster community.

Holding the meeting at the same parish also allows parish administrators to provide resources and maintenance to support the ministry. Consequently, the advantage of holding the weekly meeting at the same place usually outweighs the benefits of having multiple parishes host it on a rotating schedule.

In selecting the parish to host the weekly meeting, considerations include location, parking, church facilities (especially meeting rooms for discussion), and availability of a priest, deacon, or pastoral associate. It is also preferable to select a parish with a vibrant community and many young adults among its participants. Such vitality will help the ministry attract new participants, especially when it is first getting off the ground. Other meetings can be held at other parishes, especially at those parishes where a substantial number of ministry participants either live or attend Mass. In this way, the different Catholic entities sponsoring the 20s/30s ministry are involved in hosting its actual activities.

For example, Parish A might have a central location, a priest or deacon available for adoration on a regular basis, and adequate meeting rooms, so it would be the obvious choice for the main weekly meeting. Meanwhile, Parish B has an excellent parish center with many meetings rooms, and perhaps it could host a bible or theology study. Parish C has a well-developed community service program or social justice outreach where participants could volunteer on a regular basis. Parish D has a parish school and a gym and playing fields where there could be a weekly softball/basketball/ultimate Frisbee game. Parish E might have a thriving men's or women's group that young adults might attend together, and Parish F might have a charismatic prayer group. Parish G might have a youth ministry that could use some young adult volunteers or a religious education program that needs teachers, and ministry participants could serve these needs as a team rather than as just individuals. Participants might meet at Coffeehouse A for a monthly book club. Whatever is decided, for most events, it works better when the same parish always hosts the same event. The regularity builds stability, and the stability builds community.

For some events, however, regular location is not important. For example, an annual volleyball game might be held at a different parish every year. One-time social events, service events, spiritual events, retreats, and other gatherings can be deliberately scheduled for different parishes. Not only does this involve more parishes, it also allows the ministry to make itself better known in the host parish.

Another good way to integrate multiple parishes is a monthly Sunday Mass, followed by brunch/dinner, with the Mass hosted by a different parish every month. This rotating Mass and brunch/dinner involves many different parishes in a natural way. It also provides a natural way to publicize the ministry: at the Mass the young adults attend, the priest can make a special announcement welcoming the ministry and invite young adults present to join the 20s/30s ministry for brunch/dinner afterwards. Parishes and Masses with a large young adult attendance should be given preferential treatment in the rotating schedule, in order to reach as many young adults as possible. Evening Masses often work especially well, because they tend to attract a large number of young adults.

Coordination between multiple 20s/30s ministries in the same region

When there are multiple 20s/30s ministries in the same region or city, periodic gatherings can be desirable. The coordination can range from annual events or retreats to something more regular. The main purpose of these regional gatherings is to foster community among different ministries, and to allow young adults to make new connections and new friendships.

One option for regular collaboration is hosting a monthly gathering at some central location, perhaps the cathedral of the diocese. The meeting starts with adoration and music, and then leads to some sort of gathering and discussion afterwards. Sometimes it might be preferable to have a talk instead.

The core teams of the different 20s/30s ministries could be involved in planning and organizing these regional gatherings, perhaps on a rotating basis.

Diocesan organizational structures

Overview

Depending on the circumstances in the local Church, dioceses may want to organize a core team of young adults in order to coordinate events that serve the entire diocese. The purpose of a diocesan core team is to serve young adults on the diocesan level in a way that is not possible for individual 20s/30s ministries, or even regional clusters of 20s/30s ministries. It aims not to replace the activities and ministry of individual 20s/30s ministries, but to supplement them.

Many dioceses already have structures for overseeing young adult ministry, in which case such a core team may not be necessary or helpful. If there is an existing diocesan outreach to young adults, the leadership of local 20s/30s parish ministries should maintain regular contact and communication with those offices to ensure good collaboration.

Possible events and projects

The diocesan core team might plan events such as:

- ▶ Diocesan young adult pilgrimages or retreats
- ▶ Theology on Tap programs
- ▶ Diocesan mission trips, *e.g.*, Habitat for Humanity
- ▶ Lenten days of recollection
- ▶ Annual young adult picnic
- ▶ Annual young adult Pentecost Vigil
- ▶ Annual young adult day-long conference

It might also undertake projects to build community among young adults such as:

- Coordinating a diocesan young adult website
- Constructing an email directory of young adults
- Providing information to parishes to help them become more young adult friendly

The diocesan core team might or might not actually undertake the organization of these events and projects themselves. More likely, they will find it helpful to delegate an event or project to particular 20s/30s ministries. For example, it might be decided to have an annual young adult picnic. One particular 20s/30s ministry could host it every year (perhaps they have especially nice parish grounds), or each year a different 20s/30s ministry could host it.

Membership of the diocesan core team

The membership of this core team could be something like the following:

- Official staff representative from the diocese (i.e. young adult ministry director)
- Coordinators (or co-leaders) of local 20s/30s ministries
- Representatives from local 20s/30s ministries
- Other active Catholic young adults
- Other pastoral ministers (in ministries connected to the young adult experience)

The diocesan core team runs very similarly to the core team of an individual core team with the same emphasis on consensus decision-making. Oversight is provided by the diocesan representative, who has veto power over the deliberations of the core team. The representative ideally attends the meetings of the core teams, but if that is not possible, he or she can be given minutes of the meeting, and in this way can stay in the loop and intervene when necessary.

Unlike the membership of the core team of a local 20s/30s ministry, the membership of the diocesan core team is not open to every young adult who wants to help. The representatives sent from local 20s/30s ministry should in some way be recommended by their own core teams and/or their chaplains or directors. This requirement helps guarantee that the diocesan core team truly represents the lived reality of the various local 20s/30s ministries.

Other young adults might also be involved at the discretion of the diocesan representative. For example, there may be some young adults working in parishes in some ministerial capacity, perhaps as youth ministers, who would have exceptional gifts and abilities to contribute. They could contribute much to the discussions of the diocesan core team. They may also have a particular talent in planning diocesan-wide young adult events. A great proportion of the members, however, should be involved in local 20s/30s ministries, to ensure that the concerns of local ministries are adequately represented in its planning and discussions.

Chapter 10

Adapting This Model of Ministry to Particular Circumstances

Overview

The model proposed in this guide is meant to be adapted to particular circumstances. This chapter will discuss some common reasons a ministry might want to adapt it, discuss the pros and cons of such modifications, and then offer some suggestions for how to proceed.

Chaplains and Advisors

The 20s/30s ministry model ideally involves a priest chaplain who participates in the discussions of the core team, oversees the weekly adoration, occasionally makes himself available for confession, and is generally present at 20s/30s ministry events. Many priests, however, do not have the time to be involved. In these situations, a pastoral associate or an older lay person or religious can serve as an advisor to the ministry. It is important that the lay advisor communicate clearly and regularly with the pastor or parish leadership. Nonetheless, it is important that every 20s/30s ministry have a priest chaplain, even if he is very rarely involved in 20s/30s ministry decisions or activities. Occasionally the 20s/30s ministry will need a priest for liturgies and sacraments, and so having a go-to priest assigned to the ministry is helpful.

Since the 20s/30s ministry is sponsored by a particular parish, it is important that the pastor has some oversight over its activities. Generally speaking, this oversight boils down to veto power over plans that the pastor thinks would have negative pastoral implications. In practice, such veto power may be delegated to the chaplain or advisor who is more involved in day to day affairs.

If a lay person serves as the advisor to a ministry, it is crucial that the advisor be significantly older than the ministry's participants. Otherwise, the advisor's delegated authority could create tension on a personal level. For example, some parishes may have a young adult serving as youth minister, who is also asked to oversee young adult ministry in the parish. In this case, it does not seem advisable for the youth minister to serve as the ministry's advisor: because he or she would be a peer to the rest of the core team, or perhaps even younger than other core team members, the exercise of any oversight is likely to cause unnecessary tension.

When a chaplain is not available on a day-to-day basis, and no other advisor is available, the core team should simply proceed without much involvement from a chaplain or advisor. In such circumstances, the core team may want to submit the minutes of its meetings to the pastor as a courtesy. That way, if the pastor has any concerns he can speak to the core team. If the core team is considering anything that might have a significant impact on the parish or the 20s/30s ministry, they should contact the pastor to discuss it with him.

Adapting the model for a campus ministry

The model proposed in this guide is geared to creating a community of young adults within the context of a typical parish. A campus ministry, however, could also adapt this model to its purposes; some campus ministries have already used aspects of this model and found them helpful. If a campus ministry program is already established, the weekly meeting of the 20s/30s ministry model could add to the campus ministry's existing programs. If a campus ministry program has not yet been established, the model given here could be implemented as the core of the campus ministry's extra-liturgical programming.

Shortening the weekly meeting

According to the model given here, the weekly meeting lasts for a good three hours: an hour for adoration; an hour for the faith discussion (including moving over form the church, getting settled, making announcements, *etc.*); and then however long people socialize afterwards. In some situations, it may be preferable to shorten the weekly meeting. The easiest way to shorten the meeting is to shorten the period of adoration or allocate less time for small group discussions.

Making do without musicians for adoration

It might happen that there are a good number of young adults who would like to start a 20s/30s ministry, but they do not have a musician who can provide music for adoration. What should be done? In the experience of those who have developed this model, this element plays a crucial role in its success. For whatever reason, adoration combined with well-performed contemporary music often attracts young adults in great numbers. Other models of ministry might well thrive without contemporary music, but to reach its fullest potential, the model proposed here seems to require it. Yet if musicians cannot be found, holding silent adoration can still be useful: by creating space for communal contemplative prayer, it enhances whatever discussion comes afterward.

Naming the ministry

When the ministry is being formed, the core team should think carefully about the ministry's name. There are many advantages to a simple name like "The St. X 20s/30s ministry." Although such names are bland, they are also very descriptive and require little explanation. (It is especially helpful when the ministry's name includes the ministry's age range, because outside of church circles, many think that "young adult ministries" are for teenagers.) The fact that it is nondescript means that, while it may not have zip, it does it grate, either: the kinds of names that are most attractive to some people also tend to be off-putting to others. Alternatively, a different, less descriptive name has its own advantages, too. It gives the ministry more personality.

Chapter 11

Common Problems and Practical Suggestions

Overview

Every Christian community inevitably experiences conflict, obstacles, and unexpected challenges. This chapter will address some common issues that may develop in 20s/30s ministries and offer some practical suggestions. Two comments apply to almost everything that might come up. First, problems and tensions should not be seen as an aberration, or a sign that the ministry must be failing and on the brink of disaster. The strange thing would be if there were no problems or tensions. Second, open communication is essential. Often simply addressing some conflict or difficulty can cause it to evaporate, or at least transform it into something manageable.

Because human nature is the same everywhere, and because Christian community has features that transcend particular situations, the same problems often come up repeatedly. This chapter offers some suggestions for the problems that are likely to come up in a 20s/30s ministry. Sometimes the sheer naming of common problems can be helpful—it tells us that we are not alone—and hopefully the practical suggestions given here will also prove helpful in addressing these common problems, or in circumventing them entirely.

Disagreements and burn-out in the core team

The 20s/30s ministry depends on the core team for its flourishing. Without a well-functioning core team, the 20s/30s ministry simply cannot thrive to its fullest potential. The key to a successful core team is simple but challenging: a common commitment to unity and to looking out for each other. If this commitment is there—however imperfectly lived out—the core team will thrive.

Avoiding burn-out

The 20s/30s ministry depends on young adults taking ownership of the ministry and dividing among themselves the organizational responsibilities. Because core team responsibilities are often broadly and vaguely defined, it is easy for volunteers—who are often very generous by disposition—to take on more than they should. After a few months, or during periods of great stress, over-extension can take its toll, and then the volunteer might need to drop out entirely.

To avoid such burn-out, it is essential that core team members look out for each other. When they think somebody has too much on their plate, they should say something and offer to help. Often the people who most need assistance will be the last to ask for it. The 20s/30s ministry coordinator should be particularly attentive to this issue. For example, the ministry coordinator may sense that a member of the core team seems frazzled or overworked. In such situations, the ministry coordinator should take the initiative of talking to him or her, and seeing if he or she would like to take a step back or needs assistance from other core team members.

Lastly, although positions involve a commitment of one year, it is important that core team members keep in mind that this commitment should not cause them to hesitate dropping out if they feel that their responsibilities have become too much. Once a ministry has become established, it is usually easy to find a replacement anyway.

Balancing structure with creativity

The 20s/30s model deliberately focuses on encouraging creativity and full ownership of the ministry by the core team. The goal is to create a space where people feel free to try new ideas, even crazy ones, and see if they work—and then not particularly care if they don't. But this space for creativity can only be maintained if there is also some basic structure. This basic structure is supplied by the main weekly meeting. Therefore the core team must be very, very cautious about modifying the format of the weekly meeting. In practice, this means that any proposed modifications should have strong support from the entire core team before they are implemented. Any serious reservations by a minority indicate that it would not be good to proceed with the proposed modification. The stakes are too high to move forward without a strong consensus.

However, just because a proposal is not a good idea for the weekly meeting doesn't mean that it isn't a great idea for a different meeting. For example, some core team members might propose dropping music during adoration, even when musicians are available; or dropping the social gathering and replacing it with a communal rosary; or having lectures every week instead of faith discussion. All of these are worthy proposals, but because the weekly meeting must be oriented to serve the needs of everyone, and especially new participants and those on the margins of the Church, these adaptations (at least, in most situations) are unlikely to be beneficial. Once in a blue moon, an occasional modification might be good, but structural changes that jeopardize the weekly meeting's ability to meet a wide range of pastoral needs should not be entertained.

Guarding the integrity of the weekly meeting also minimizes disagreements in the core team. Even when core team members would be strongly opposed to a particular modification of the weekly meeting, they might be very supportive of the same idea in a different context. Keeping the format of the weekly meeting constant also encourages creativity. Everybody knows that the weekly meeting will "always be there," so that if some experimental activity flops, it won't impact the vitality of the ministry, and so people feel more freedom to experiment.

Handling disagreement

The core team's decision-making process is designed to surface disagreement, provoke discussion, and then lead the core team to reach decisions that everybody can support or at least accept. The purpose of the discussion is not simply to decide between multiple options. In the course of the discussion, the ministry may come to see new possibilities. Or it may recognize that a majority-supported proposal needs to incorporate the concerns of the minority. In short, disagreement itself is not a problem. It is a sign that people feel comfortable voicing what they really think, and that the core team is working toward a solution that will satisfy as many concerns as possible.

Still, disagreement can become a problem if it is not handled properly. To prevent disagreements from leading to resentment, core team members should guard against pushing forward their opinions stridently; make an effort to listen to what others say; and exhibit a readiness to withdraw their objections when a proposal generates a groundswell of support from others. Furthermore, when one member feels that another core team member's behavior is problematic, it is important that he or she address the issue sooner rather than later, taking counsel from others if necessary. Minor disagreements can become a source of major tension if they are not addressed promptly. Christ gives very practical advice about how to go about resolving disagreement (see Mt 18:15-20), and his words emphasize the importance of raising concerns directly with the person involved.

Personality clashes, conflicts, and disagreements are inevitable, and that means there will be a constant need for forgiveness. It has been said that the ideal Christian community is one where we can forgive and be forgiven. When there is a combination of frank discussion of conflict and a readiness to forgive, the most serious internal problems can be avoided.

Dealing with problematic personalities

It may happen that somebody joins the core team who, for whatever reason, is very disruptive, and single-handedly creates many internal problems. In such circumstances, core team members may wish to consult with each other, and especially with the chaplain or advisor, to assess the situation. Every effort should be made to see if the individual can be gently corrected and made to see how his or her behavior has been disruptive, in the hope that the individual will improve and be able to continue on the core team. In more serious cases, or if such a correction is not effective, it may be necessary to ask the individual not to attend core team meetings, at least for a period of time. If the chaplain or advisor is involved in the day-to-day activities of the 20s/30s ministry, he or she may be the natural person for this delicate task.

Welcoming new members with special needs or challenging personalities

Since the central purpose of the 20s/30s ministry is to create a Christ-centered community of young adults, an atmosphere of welcome and hospitality are especially important. Consequently, young adults should give special thought to welcoming newcomers with special needs or challenging personalities.

Child care

Single parents and married couples may feel inhibited from attending 20s/30s ministry meetings if they do not have easy access to child care. To make it easier for new participants with infants or small children to join, the core team may want to arrange child care, especially during the weekly meeting. Other parishioners, especially those involved with the parish youth ministry (participants and leaders), may be happy to assist.

Welcoming challenging personalities

A warm welcome is easy to extend when new participants are interesting, amiable, well put-together, and ready to contribute to the ministry. But if the ministry is successful in cultivating a healthy Christ-centered community, new participants will inevitably come along who are attracted by the 20s/30s ministry community partly because they find it much more difficult than the average person to find a warm welcome. In the concrete encounter with such persons, the ministry has a special and defining opportunity to welcome Christ. If it meets this challenge, not only will the ministry gain a new participant, but the ministry's charity and fellowship will deepen in ways that will enrich everybody. If it fails to seize this opportunity, the ministry will slowly but surely drift toward becoming a Christian clique. The ministry depends on the core team to set the tone. If core team members make an effort to extend a warm welcome to all comers, even if some young adults are not able to follow their example, such (understandable and inevitable) individual failures will not harm the ministry's spirit.

By the same token, the ministry should not tolerate inappropriate behavior or enable psychological pathology. Sometimes generous young adults may feel an obligation to cater to somebody's neediness in ways that are unhelpful to everybody involved. Such persons may need to be encouraged to maintain firm personal boundaries, and to realize that they cannot solve all of the needy person's problems nor should they try. Because situations are often complex and confusing, when problems and questions arise, young adults may want to take counsel with each other, and especially with the ministry's chaplain and/or advisor.

Ministries should be particularly cautious about the possibility that older men may be attracted to ministry events, and may pose as being younger than they are, because they are drawn by the younger women in the ministry. Sometimes this is innocent: an older man might attend ministry events, for example, not realizing that there is an upper age limit. Nonetheless, many ministries have reported problems with older men attending ministry events and behaving inappropriately toward the women in the ministry. Sometimes such men are obviously socially awkward, sometimes they are not. It is a frequent problem among young adult ministries, and it can have significantly disruptive consequences. It can be avoided by enforcing the ministry's upper age limit.

Aging-out

One of the most challenging issues of young adult ministry is what to do when participants have grown older than a particular ministry's age range. While many young adults will have moved on from the ministry for a variety of reasons—other interests, new job, marriage, children, *etc.*—

before they become too old for the ministry, many young adults may not find it easy to move on, especially if many of their younger friends are still involved in the 20s/30s ministry.

Every ministry will need to decide for itself how to negotiate this difficult dilemma, balancing sensitivity to persons with fidelity to its identity. Perhaps the most important is to make sure that the ministry's connection to parish life is always implicitly emphasized. Such emphasis will help participants become more grounded in parish life during the course of their involvement with the ministry, and thus afterwards more able to find other ways to be involved in the life of the parish. Furthermore, if enough participants are aging-out around the same time, it may be possible to establish another ministry (*e.g.*, a reading club, a discussion ministry, a men's or women's group, *etc.*) that gives them an alternative ecclesial context. Young adults who have aged out can be a valuable resource for helping parishes develop ministries that they might otherwise not be able to create or sustain, such as forming small groups, or developing an evangelization team. If the adoration portion of the 20s/30s ministry meeting is open to the parish—as it ideally should be—other ministries could join the 20s/30s ministry for the adoration, and then meet separately afterwards. Additionally, ministries can make the age range very clear, perhaps by incorporating it into the ministry's name. Age-explicit names remove the expectation that it would be appropriate to remain involved in the ministry indefinitely, and thus encourage people to plan ahead—and perhaps start another ministry.

Chapter 12

Final Thoughts

The aspiration that humanity nurtures, amid countless injustices and sufferings, is the hope of a new civilization marked by freedom and peace. But for such an undertaking, a new generation of builders is needed. Moved not by fear or violence but by the urgency of genuine love, they must learn to build, brick by brick, the city of God within the city of man.

Allow me, dear young people, to consign this hope of mine to you: you must be those "builders"! You are the men and women of tomorrow. The future is in your hearts and in your hands. God is entrusting to you the task, at once difficult and uplifting, of working with him in the building of the civilization of love.

– Pope John Paul II, Toronto, July 2002.

Community is one of the most pressing felt needs among young adults, and community is something that the Church can provide like no other society or institution. The Church is the mystical body of Christ, and it has been entrusted with the Word of God, with Christ's new commandment of loving service, and above all with the Eucharist. It is the fullest expression of the home and communion that is sought by all, but especially the young.

There is no question that the Church has something to offer today's young adults, and there are many reasons for hope, for encouragement, and for confidence in God's continuing action. This guide is offered as a resource for all those who desire to help young adults claim their full place in the Church.

Appendix A

Detailed Descriptions of Different Core Team Positions

Overview

Some core team positions are essential to every 20s/30s ministry, such as ministry coordinator, chaplain, and secretary. Other positions are established according to the needs of a particular ministry. For example, it is ideal to have a service coordinator who is assisted by a service committee. Yet when a ministry is starting, there may not even be a service coordinator, let alone a service committee, but simply one core team member who organizes both social and service events. Similarly, it is ideal to have a separate treasurer, especially if the ministry has a budget from the parish, but in many circumstances the secretary could also serve as the ministry's treasurer. Moreover, if the ministry decides to add another meeting or regular activity (*e.g.*, a women's bible study), there will need to be a core team member assigned to take charge of it.

The rule of thumb is to divide responsibilities as much as possible. This has a number of positive effects. Nobody is overburdened, core team members feel more ownership of the ministry, and the ministry does not fall apart if somebody has to take a step back.

Generally, when a core team is first starting, there are usually a minimal number of positions. Then, gradually, as the core team expands, the positions are multiplied to spread the growing responsibilities more manageably.

What follows are descriptions of different core team positions. They may or may not be appropriate for a particular 20s/30s ministry at a particular stage of its growth. They are meant to give a sense of how tasks might be divided. The actual composition of the core team, and how the responsibilities are divided, should be formed in response to particular needs and circumstances.

Core team position descriptions

Ministry coordinator/Co-Coordinator

The coordinator (and/or co-coordinator) is the ministry's "wide-angle lens" and its primary symbol of unity. It is the ministry coordinator's responsibility to lead by word and example. He or she serves as representative of the ministry when necessary and keeps an eye out to make sure that issues and problems that arise are dealt with judiciously. He or she also looks out for other core team members, especially if they start to seem overburdened. The ministry coordinator(s) should be in close contact with the chaplain and/or advisor, especially when some concern or difficulty surfaces, as well as the pastor.

- ▶ Works to ensure that the 20s/30s ministry and especially the 20s/30s ministry core team run smoothly and maintain a spirit of unity

- ▶ Leads the weekly meeting

- ▶ Sends out weekly email announcements

- ▶ Sets times and locations for core team meetings

- ▶ Participates in decisions and meetings of the core team

Advice for 20s/30s Ministry coordinators

It should be emphasized that the 20s/30s ministry coordinator is a demanding position. It requires a great deal of prudence, patience, and charity. In view of its special demands, here is some good advice from a former 20s/30s ministry coordinator:

- ▶ You can't go wrong being nice to people.

- ▶ Delegate as much as possible because there will always be more than enough for you to do.

- ▶ Having someone to confide in is very helpful. This may even be someone outside the ministry who can give you an objective perspective.

▶ Be present. Attend as many ministry events as possible. This is the best way to get to know people and develop good rapport, which always helps when resolving conflicts/crises.

▶ No matter how hard you try, you cannot be all things to all people. Be able to deliver bad news.

Chaplain

The chaplain oversees the ministry's connection to the parish, and ensures provision of the ministry's sacramental needs. To the extent possible, the chaplain is also involved in the activities of the 20s/30s ministry, and especially the core team. Because the chaplain can be present to the ministry without being fully part of it, they can provide an important outlet for the ministry. People often feel more comfortable confiding in them about problems in the ministry or core team. They also have a special vantage point from which to observe ministry dynamics and offer suggestions when necessary. To safeguard this special role, the chaplain should make every effort to avoid compromising their perceived objectivity.

▶ Presides and preaches at weekly adoration, perhaps in rotation with other priests or deacons

▶ Provides occasional opportunities for the Sacrament of Reconciliation

▶ Serves as liaison to the parish staff

▶ Oversees doctrinal and pastoral issues as they arise

▶ Oversees 20s/30s ministry retreat planning

▶ Organizes occasional special events (especially spiritual events)

▶ Provides advice to core team members as questions arise

▶ Participates in decisions and meetings of the core team

Advisor

The chaplain's role can be supplemented by a religious or lay advisor. In situations where a chaplain only provides sacramental ministry, the chaplain's non-sacramental responsibilities are filled by the advisor.

Secretary

The secretary serves the core team by preparing the agenda, leading the actual meetings of the core team, and then afterwards distributing the minutes.

  ▶ Sends out an email to see if anyone has agenda items

  ▶ Prepares agenda

  ▶ Runs core team meetings and takes minutes

  ▶ Reads minutes and verifies that core team members are implementing decisions

  ▶ Participates in decisions and meetings of the core team

Treasurer

The treasurer manages the ministry's funds, pays vendors, and liaises with parish staff as necessary, especially if the ministry's budget is managed by the parish business manager.

  ▶ Oversees use of annual budget and fundraising

  ▶ Serves as a liaison with the business manager of the parish

  ▶ Participates in decisions and meetings of the core team

Music Coordinator

Typically a musician, the music coordinator ensures that there is music as often as possible at the weekly adoration. He or she recruits musicians, arrange schedules, provides music materials, and prepares whatever equipment is necessary.

- ▸ Prepares music and facilities for weekly adoration

- ▸ Organizes and distributes the schedule of musicians for weekly adoration

- ▸ Sends quarterly email to interested people (who have responded to call for musicians) asking for volunteers to lead music or to sing/play with a music leader

- ▸ Copies and distributes song lyrics if needed

- ▸ Participates in decisions and meetings of the core team

Faith Discussion Coordinator

The faith discussion coordinator oversees the rotating schedule of faith discussion. He or she makes sure that facilities and any special require-ments are provided, recruits small group discussion leaders, and is ready to lead the weekly meeting if the ministry coordinator (or co-coordinator) is unavailable. This coordinator may take charge of one of the four weekly formats.

- ▸ Schedules meeting locations and sets up room for meeting

- ▸ Assists ministry coordinator with leading weekly meetings when necessary

- ▸ Coordinates with other core team members associated with the weekly meeting (i.e., the music coordinator, the presentation coordinator, etc.)

- ▸ Informs ministry coordinator(s) of the need for schedule changes (*e.g.*, when there is a conflict with parish facilities)

- ▸ Coordinates small group leaders, recruits new leaders, and provides training sessions if necessary (sometimes by arranging sessions with a member of the parish staff)

- ▸ Participates in decisions and meetings of the core team

Presentation Coordinator (1st Week)

The presentation coordinator oversees the monthly talk by a visiting speaker. Ideally, the speaker coordinator is assisted by a committee that meets 2–3 times per year to plan the selection of speakers and topics.

- ▶ Coordinates topic and speaker selection for the 1st week

- ▶ Arranges planning meetings of a lecture committee 2–3 times per year

- ▶ Executes decisions of the lecture selection meetings after consulting with chaplain

- ▶ Introduces speakers before their talks

- ▶ Keeps an eye out for new and interesting speakers

- ▶ Works with treasurer to provide compensation for each speaker, if possible

- ▶ Participates in decisions and meetings of the core team

Scripture Discussion Coordinator (2nd Week)

This coordinator oversees the Scripture Discussion format. Ideally, he or she prepares discussion questions in advance and then consults with the chaplain or advisor for feedback, in order to make discussion questions as effective as possible.

- ▶ Coordinates Scripture Discussion format

- ▶ Prepares discussion questions for the Scripture Discussion in consultation with the chaplain and/or advisor

- ▶ Distributes and gathers scripture readings and questions if necessary

- ▶ Participates in decisions and meetings of the core team

Reflection Coordinator (3rd Week)

This coordinator oversees the reflection and the discussion afterwards. He or she recruits volunteers from the ministry and helps volunteers to prepare their talks by reviewing the message and offering constructive feedback. The coordinator is also responsible for preparing questions for the discussion after the talk.

- ▶ Coordinates Reflection and Discussion format
- ▶ Reviews and discusses reflections with speaker prior to meeting
- ▶ Prepares questions for the discussion and makes copies
- ▶ Participates in decisions and meetings of the core team

Theology Discussion Coordinator (4th Week)

This coordinator prepares the material for the monthly theology discussion. He or she either selects the text and prepares the discussion questions or finds an appropriate study guide. Ideally, the materials are prepared in advance with consultation from the chaplain and/or advisor.

- ▶ Prepares or selects the texts and discussion questions
- ▶ Prepares and distributes materials
- ▶ Participates in decisions and meetings of the core team

Small Group Leaders

Small group leaders are "on call" to lead discussions at weekly meetings. They can remove their name from the list of willing leaders at any time. They may or may not be part of the core team; many young adults may be happy to lead small group discussions, but would rather not be involved in the core team.

- ▶ Available at weekly meetings to lead a small group discussion
- ▶ If they wish, participate in decisions and meetings of the core team

Bible Study / Theology Study Coordinator

This coordinator organizes various study cycles of the bible or theology throughout the year. Before each 3–6 week cycle, the coordinator arranges for an open meeting to decide the topic and materials. The coordinator also recruits volunteers to host the meetings and emails reminders with directions to the 20s/30s ministry.

- ▶ Coordinates the various study cycles
- ▶ Arranges organizational meeting to select topic and materials
- ▶ Finds participants to host each study cycle in their homes
- ▶ Sends weekly email to remind 20s/30s ministry with topic and directions
- ▶ Leads study or finds a leader
- ▶ Participates in decisions and meetings of the core team

Social Chairperson

The social chairperson is in charge of arranging the various social events during the year. Ideally there is a committee that assists in the planning and execution of these events. Often the social chairperson needs to recruit volunteers to help with individual events or to bring food and drink.

Ministry participants will often come forward to organize various social events, some spontaneously, some with more planning. The social chairperson may want to help them in some way, but such above-and-beyond help is not the responsibility of the social chairperson. The social chairperson should, however, do what he or she can to foster an atmosphere where people feel comfortable and encouraged to come forward and organize their own ideas for events.

- ▶ Chairs social committee, which may meet multiple times to plan social events
- ▶ Coordinates and organizes official 20s/30s ministry-sponsored social events

- ▸ Coordinates monthly Sunday Mass and brunch/dinner
- ▸ Coordinates food and games for receptions
- ▸ Keeps an eye out for opportunities to integrate with parish social events
- ▸ Participates in decisions and meetings of the core team

Service Chairperson

The service chairperson investigates and arranges the practical details of various kinds of service and social justice work. Ideally he or she is assisted by a committee that helps with the planning and execution of service events throughout the year.

- ▸ Chairs service committee
- ▸ Coordinates and organizes opportunities for service through regular forms of service and quarterly events
- ▸ Encourages interested ministry participants to lead service events
- ▸ Keeps an eye out for opportunities to integrate with parish service events
- ▸ Participates in decisions and meetings of the core team

Public Relations Chairperson

The public relations chairperson oversees the 20s/30s ministry relationship with the wider church and the surrounding community. This takes two main forms. The first is the publicizing the 20s/30s ministry among young adults, parishes, the diocese, and the community. The second is networking and building relationships with various ecclesial communities.

- ▸ Chairs public relations committee
- ▸ Works with committee and the webmaster to publicize the 20s/30s ministry and design and distribute various forms of promotional materials

- Coordinates outreach to young adults in the parish and archdiocese

- Coordinates speaking about the ministry at local parishes

- Networks with other young adult ministries in the area, local campus ministries, and the diocesan office for young adult ministry

- Distributes information to local parishes and the diocese about the ministry, especially as a major special event approaches

- Keeps the local diocese updated about the ministry's meetings and events, so that the diocese can distribute the information to others via the diocese's website, parish communications, emails, *etc.*

- Participates in decisions and meetings of the core team

Webmaster/Social Media Coordinator

The webmaster/social media coordinator maintains and updates the 20s/30s ministry website and social media pages. The webmaster should set realistic goals about how frequently he or she can update the website, and then structure the materials on the website accordingly. For example, if the webmaster does not have time to update the website regularly, the 20s/30s ministry should not attempt to provide a very detailed calendar of events on the website.

- Oversees and updates the website and social media pages regularly

- Adds pictures of events to website and social media pages

- Updates the website's calendar of events

- Participates in decisions and meetings of the core team

Welcome Committee

The purpose of the welcome committee is to make everyone feel welcome in the 20s/30s ministry. The committee gathers the contact information of new participants at the weekly meeting, contacts new participants with information about the ministry, and organizes an annual social gathering to welcome new participants. Committee members might also stand at the entrance of the discussion portion of the weekly meeting and greet young adults as they enter.

- ▶ Makes effort to welcome everyone, new and old, at meetings

- ▶ Collects email addresses from new participants at weekly meetings

- ▶ Extends welcome to "lost participants" of the contact list by email or phone

- ▶ Organizes annual or semi-annual party to welcome new participants

- ▶ Participates in decisions and meetings of the core team

Members-at-Large

Members-at-Large are core team members who attend core team meetings and participate in discussions and decisions, but do not have a particular position. Often they serve as all-purpose volunteers who step up to serve in a variety of capacities. They may also serve on different committee within the ministry.

- ▶ Assists the ministry in a variety of ways

- ▶ May serve on internal committees

- ▶ Participates in decisions and meetings of the core team

Appendix B

Prayer Intentions for Silent Adoration

By Fr. Hugh Vincent Dyer, O.P.
Used with permission.

Prayer Intentions for the Young People of the World

You are invited to pray in silence for these and any other intentions you may have for young people. We gather to pray especially for those who do not pray for themselves that the young people of the world will be transformed and led to a life of true happiness.

(For spoken litanies, respond "Lord have mercy" after each petition)

- ▶ For young people who do not yet know the love of Christ, that the Church would bring them His love.

- ▶ For young people who do not know they have a mother in Mary.

- ▶ For young people who have been inadequately taught about the Gospel and gifts of our tradition.

- ▶ For Christian young people that the Holy Spirit will renew within them the graces of Baptism and Confirmation.

- ▶ For young people who have fallen away from the practice of faith.

- ▶ For the young people of the world who are orphans living on the streets and for those who are without the necessities of life: food, clean water, clothing, shelter.

- ▶ For young people who are forced into slavery and prostitution and for those whose work is unrewarding.

- ▶ For the young who live in war torn areas of the world especially those who have never known days of peace.

- ▶ For young people who suffer because of racism and prejudice.

- ▶ For young immigrants struggling to learn a new language and way of life.

- For young people who suffer from severe boredom and are in need of the interior life of Faith.

- For young people who lack genuine affirmation and for those who feel totally alone.

- For young people who suffer anxiety, depression, and other forms of mental illness.

- For young people who are considering suicide and for those who practice forms of mutilation.

- For young people who are grieving the loss of a loved one.

- For young people who suffer from terminal illness.

- For young people who suffer from learning and physical disabilities.

- For young people who are burdened by debt and financial troubles.

- For young people who are enslaved to addictions, especially those caught by drugs and alcohol.

- For young people who find their community in gangs and other criminal associations.

- For young people caught by the allure of materialism and fame.

- For young people who are in bondage to excessive entertainment and the tyranny of fads and fashion.

- For young people in bondage to pornography and other forms of sexual addiction.

- For young people that they will be given the virtue of chastity and that they will come to know that a more chaste society is a more just society.

- For young people who are caught in practices of the occult and Satanic worship.

- ▶ For young people who have been physically, emotionally, sexually, or psychologically abused.

- ▶ For young women who have had an abortion and for those who are considering one.

- ▶ For young men who have lost a child through abortion and for those who are considering participation in abortion.

- ▶ For young mothers who are raising children alone.

- ▶ For young people serving in the military.

- ▶ For young people who suffer because of a broken home.

- ▶ For Divine protection upon all young people who are vulnerable in any way.

- ▶ For young people who are searching for their vocation in life.

- ▶ For young men and women who are seeking a Christian spouse.

- ▶ For young priests and religious who are struggling with their vocation.

- ▶ For young married couples who are struggling with the challenges of life and parenthood.

- ▶ For young married couples who are having difficulty conceiving, those seeking to adopt, and for those with special needs children.

- ▶ For young single people trying to embrace the fullness of Christian life as single people.

- ▶ For young people in the legal and medical professions that they will fight to uphold the dignity of human life in all its stages.

Loving Father, grant all your children the virtues necessary for their condition and state in life, heal and liberate them according to their needs. We ask this through our Lord Jesus Christ your Son who lives and reigns with you in the unity of the Holy Spirit, one God, forever and ever. AMEN!

Prayer Intentions for the Poor

You are invited to pray in silence for these and any intentions you may have for the poor of the world. We join together in solidarity with the poor to pray for them. The Lord hears the cry of the poor. We cry out to the Lord especially for those who do not pray for themselves.

▸ For the poor who do not yet know Christ.

▸ For the poor that they will come to know Mary as their mother and advocate.

▸ For the Christian community that it will ever increase its outreach to the poor.

▸ For all who work among the poor that they will be blessed with the gift of perseverance.

▸ For Christians who are fearful of the poor that they may come to see the suffering of Christ in the poor and move to embrace the poor in genuine friendship.

▸ For the conversion of the enemies of Christ's poor who would seek to eliminate them rather than to serve them.

▸ For the conversion of creditors and all others who take advantage of the poor for material gain.

▸ For the poor who do not yet know their dignity as children of God.

▸ For the poor who lack the necessities of life: food, clothing, shelter and clean water.

▸ For poor pregnant women who are considering abortion that they may find hope through the Church.

▸ For poor single parents.

▸ For poor parents who are raising large families.

▸ For poor parents who are trying to raise children in the midst of violent neighborhoods.

▸ For poor parents who are raising mentally or physically disabled children.

▸ For poor immigrants who work to support their families here and abroad.

▸ For the poor who are taken advantage of for the sake of political gain.

▸ For the poor who receive wages inadequate to support a family.

▸ For the poor who live with massive financial debt.

▸ For the poor who have missed opportunities for education.

▸ For the poor who seek false hope in gambling, the lottery, and dealing drugs.

▸ For the poor who suffer from addiction to drugs and alcohol.

▸ For poor women and children who suffer from abusive relationships.

▸ For poor children who have been abandoned by one or both parents.

▸ For the elderly poor who have no one to care for them.

▸ For the poor who get lost in excessive entertainment and meaningless frivolity.

▸ For migrant workers especially those who have been maimed using farm equipment.

▸ For the poor who are sick and those who do not have adequate health care.

▸ For the poor who face frustrating paperwork and daunting bureaucracies in order to have their needs answered.

▸ For the poor who make their homes among the garbage dumps of the world.

▸ For the mentally ill homeless who wander our streets.

- For the poor whose life of want has led them to crime and prison.
- For the poor who have been driven to a life of prostitution.
- For those who remain poor because of racial injustice or war.
- For the poor who suffer embarrassment because of their poverty.
- For the poor who have been given over to debilitating anger that they will come to peace and the hope for a better future.
- For the poor who are unable to rest on the Sabbath because of financial constraints.
- For the poor who find it difficult to answer the call to priesthood or the consecrated life because of material want.
- St. Vincent de Paul — *Pray for us*
- Bl. Teresa of Calcutta — *Pray for us*
- St. Lawrence — *Pray for us*
- All you Patrons of the Poor — *Pray for us*

Almighty God, Father of the Poor, grant to your poor the virtues necessary for their lives and provide for all their needs. May we who receive the Body and Blood of your Son be strengthened to render faithful and generous service to the poor. We ask this through Jesus Christ your son who became poor for our sake.

AMEN!

Prayer Intentions for Respect Life Month

We gather to pray in silence for a greater respect for life among members of the human family. We pray for all those whose life and quality of life is threatened by sin and false views of the human person. We pray especially for those who do not pray for themselves. Please add any petitions you may have.

- ▶ For the virtue of gratitude to be given to all people.

- ▶ For Christians to be given courage to live their Christian vocation as an adventure of life and love.

- ▶ For Catholics, that in eating the Body and Blood of the Lord they will be moved to give of themselves in service to those who are most vulnerable.

- ▶ For a return to meditation on the Crucified Christ as a means for gaining sensitivity toward the suffering of others.

- ▶ For young married men and women that they will be open and generous in the call to have children and for those who are seeking to adopt children.

- ▶ For an end to abortion and for the conversion of doctors who perform abortions.

- ▶ For the Sisters of Life and all consecrated persons who are dedicated to promoting the dignity of human life.

- ▶ For all who give of their time and resources in the cause of defending life.

- ▶ For the unborn that our society will respect their dignity as persons from the moment of conception.

- ▶ For baby girls in China and India who face the threat of sex-selected abortion.

- ▶ For babies who are threatened by abortion because of Down's syndrome and other birth defects.

- For young men and women who are considering the possibility of abortion that their hearts be turned from fear to love.

- For all those who live under the threats of terror, violence, and war.

- For all who suffer from racism and for the survivors of genocide, especially the people of Rwanda, Kenya, and the Sudan.

- For those who are considering suicide that they will be given hope.

- For those whose lives are made difficult by physical or mental disabilities.

- For an end to the death penalty and for all prisoners on death row that their hearts will be turned to the love of Christ.

- For the success of stem-cell technologies developed with respect for human life.

- For a deeper awareness of the call to unite our sufferings with the sufferings of Christ for the salvation of the world.

- For those who do not have adequate health care and for doctors who provide generous and free service.

- For all who suffer a loss of hope, especially those who are lonely.

- For elderly people who suffer in poorly run nursing homes and institutions.

- For elderly, comatose, and terminally ill people who live under the threat of euthanasia.

- For the people of the world who live under threat of famine due to political machinations.

- For a more just distribution of the world's goods.

- For an increase of respect for the value of chastity in promoting the common good.

▶ For women and children who suffer from various forms of abuse.

▶ For an end to the gratuitous portrayal of violence and sex in television and movies.

▶ For the success of film, theater, literature, music, architecture, and art that encourage the human spirit and foster a respect for life and authentic human culture.

▶ For those who work is boring, difficult, or unrewarding.

▶ For those who are considering divorce that they be given the virtues necessary for forgiveness and perseverance.

▶ For medical professionals and law makers that they will have the courage to defend life.

▶ St. Gerard Majella — *Pray for us*

▶ St. Gianna Beretta Molla — *Pray for us*

▶ St. Maximilian Kolbe — *Pray for us*

▶ All you patrons of Life — *Pray for us*

Eternal Father, look with mercy upon our human culture and raise up saints in our Church to give prophetic witness to the sanctity of all human life. We ask this through Christ our Lord.

AMEN!

Random Question Ideas for Weekly Meetings

By Lisa Fiamingo. Used with permission from "Path of Grace" Spirit & Truth Guide.

The following ice breaker questions can be used during introductions at weekly meetings:

- Describe one item of clothing you love but probably should throw away.

- What toothpaste do you use? What deodorant do you use?

- What is the color of your toothbrush?

- If you could have any super power what would it be?

- What movie best describes your life?

- If you could be a fly on the wall of anyone's house, who's would it be?

- If you could be stuck in the elevator with anyone who would you choose? (dead or alive)

- Favorite toy growing up.

- Favorite song you jam out too when no one is looking.

- What was your first car? Did it have a name?

- Name a pet peeve you have.

- What is something about you that your parents would probably say is annoying?

- Favorite holiday tradition. Favorite meal for holiday season.

- Holiday tradition that your family has that you think is cool.

- When you were a kid, what did you want to be when you grew up?

▶ What cereal did you beg your parents for when walking down the cereal aisle as a child?

▶ What cartoons did you have to watch when growing up?

▶ What's your favorite 80's style?

▶ What song gets stuck in your head and you can't get it out?

▶ What food is not appetizing to you but is appetizing to most other people?

▶ Favorite expression?

▶ What was a gift that you knew you would re-gift as soon as you opened it?

Annual Survey

Adapted from a survey used by the
St. Gertrude's 20s Group (Cincinnati, Ohio).

20s/30s Ministry Survey

We really appreciate your presence! It would be very helpful to have your honest feedback to each question below!

What do you think is going well? _____

_____

_____

_____

What do you think needs improvement? _____

_____

_____

_____

What other ideas do you have? _____

_____

_____

_____

Name (optional):_____

Additional comments: _____

_____

_____

_____

_____

_____

_____

_____

_____

_____

_____

_____

_____

_____

_____

_____

_____

_____

_____

Resources for Catholic Young Adult Ministry

Sons and Daughters of the Light: This document is the US Bishops' 1996 pastoral plan for young adult ministry. It is filled with both theological insights and practical suggestions.

> usccb.org/beliefs-and-teachings/who-we-teach/young-adults/
> sons-and-daughters-of-light.cfm

Connecting Young Adults to Catholic Parishes: This resource document, developed by the USCCB Committee for Laity, Marriage, Family Life and Youth (2010), is a compilation of strategies and best practices in carrying out the bishop's vision for Young Adult Ministry, as outlined in Sons and Daughters.

> http://www.usccbpublishing.org/productdetails.cfm?sku=5-546

Young Adult Ministry in a Box: This subscription service offers a wide range of resources for reaching young adults, establishing parish-based young adult programs, and making parishes more young adult friendly. Developed by a team of experts, it is a joint initiative of NCYAMA and Busted Halo.

> http://www.youngadultministryinabox.com/

Pentecost Vigil Celebrations for 20s & 30s: This website gives information and resources for hosting diocesan (or parish) celebrations of the Pentecost Vigil for young adults. Celebrations ideally include gatherings of young adult leaders from around the diocese. Promotion of the Pentecost Vigil is a joint initiative of The Catholic University of America and the National Catholic Young Adult Ministry Association (NCYAMA).

> http://www.pentecost20s30s.com

The Changing Spirituality of Emerging Adults: this extensive research project, now housed with The Catholic University of America, looked at trends of young adults in the United States, to provide religious leaders with information on how to better minister to those in their 20s and 30s. It includes essays, research, commentaries, and case studies.

http://archives.lib.cua.edu/findingaid/changspir.cfm#IDA5AX4B

Emerging Models of Pastoral Leadership: This ten-year project, a joint effort of several national Catholic organizations, offers research and recommendations on the best practices and principles for effective, evangelizing parishes in the 21st Century. One of the primary focus areas was the pathway of young adults into Catholic leadership, outlined in its Next Generation initiatives.

http://www.usccb.org/upload/lem-summit-2015-next-gen-emerging-models-report.pdf

Links to Catholic organizations and institutions that serve young adults

United States Conference of Catholic Bishops (USCCB): Within the USCCB Secretariat for Laity, Marriage, Family Life and Youth, young adult ministry is a focus area of the U.S. bishops that aids dioceses and Catholic leaders on the ministry and outreach to young adults; *additional services also include training, networking, advocating, and resourcing those who minister with young adults.*

http://www.usccb.org/beliefs-and-teachings/who-we-teach/young-adults/index.cfm

World Youth Day USA (WYDUSA): The national initiative of the USCCB focused on promoting, preparing, resourcing, and networking pastoral leaders across the United States in their World Youth Day efforts, both locally (stateside) and internationally. (It should be noted that, despite the name, "World Youth Day" is aimed at men and women, ages 16 to 35 with a *particular focus on young adults in their 20s and 30s*).

http://www.wydusa.org

La RED (National Catholic Network de Pastoral Juvenil Hispana): An association of Catholic organizations and pastoral ministers committed to the evangelization, holistic development, and ongoing support and formation of Hispanic/Latino youth and young adults in the United States

http://www.laredpjh.org

Theology on Tap: The organizational network of the wildly successful Theology on Tap program (speakers, catechesis, formation, and evangelization for young adults, often in a secular setting), coordinated by Renew International.

http://www.renewtot.org/

Busted Halo: A Catholic media resource for young adults and ministry leaders, looking at the bringing the joy of the Gospel to all people in innovative and creative ways (through articles, video, podcasts, radio, and social media tools), sponsored by The Paulist Fathers.

http://bustedhalo.com/

Charis Ministries: A nationwide Ignatian-based retreat program for those in their 20s and 30s, with retreats held all over the country (on different aspects of Catholic life and Ignatian spirituality), sponsored by the Chicago-Detroit Province of the Society of Jesus (the Jesuits).

http://www.charisministries.org/

Christus Ministries: An Ignatian-based ministry development initiative to help parishes form young adults in discipleship and vocation, endorsed by the California Province of the Society of Jesus (the Jesuits), in partnership with the Sisters of Charity of the Incarnate Word in Houston.

http://www.christusministries.org/

Hearts on Fire: A traveling Jesuit-based retreat program for young adults, sponsored by the Apostleship of Prayer worldwide network.

http://apostleshipofprayer.org/hearts-on-fire/

Young Catholic Professionals: A nationwide network of Catholics in their 20s and 30s working in various professions, to empower young adults to witness to their faith at work and through work, and to engage young leaders in the Church.

http://www.youngcatholicprofessionals.org/

Catholic Apostolate Center: A multi-dimensional resource center, developed by the Society of the Catholic Apostolate (Pallottines) for developing formation and training programs for Church leadership in the New Evangelization and pastoral collaboration, with outreach efforts for young adult ministries.

http://www.catholicapostolatecenter.org/

Catholic Match Institute: Interactive website for singles, young engaged and married couples, and Church leaders who minister with singles and young couples, featuring articles, resources, and tools for fostering healthy relationships and marriages.

http://institute.catholicmatch.com/

Catholics on Call: A young adult vocation awareness program dedicated to helping Catholic young adults discern God's call in their lives – pointing them towards pathways to the priesthood, religious/consecrated life, lay ecclesial ministry, and active engagement in the life of the Church.

http://www.catholicsoncall.org/

National Catholic Singles Conference: Annual gathering of Catholic singles (including both young adults and older adult singles), sponsored by the Theology of the Body International Alliance and the Catholic Match Institute.

http://www.nationalcatholicsingles.com/

Knights of Columbus College & Young Adult Outreach: An initiative of the Knights of Columbus to connect with and engage Catholic young adult men in college and in their 20s and 30s.

http://www.kofc.org/un/en/college/index.html